The Second (R)evolution

The Second (R)evolution

Afrikanerdom and the Crisis of Identity

Willem de Klerk

Jonathan Ball Publishers
JOHANNESBURG

All rights reserved. No part of this publication may be reproduced or transmitted, in any form or by any means, without permission.

© Willem de Klerk

First published in 1984 by Jonathan Ball Publishers
P O Box 548
Bergvlei
2012 Johannesburg

ISBN 0 86850 083 6

Design and phototypesetting by Book Productions, Johannesburg
Printed and bound by National Book Printers, Goodwood, Cape

Contents

Introduction	2
1 The (R)evolution of Political Attitudes	6
2 The (R)evolution of Political Policy	30
3 The (R)evolution of Religious Attitudes	47
4 The (R)evolution and Afrikaner Organisations	56
5 The (R)evolution and the Afrikaans Press	68
Postscript	79

Introduction

Can it be said that an Afrikaner revolution is on the verge of breakthrough? Or is it perhaps evolution in a hurry? Some people even speak of devolution, and for those who feel that this is perhaps too harsh a judgement, the term stagnation is accepted as an accurate reflection of the Afrikaner situation.

The devolution/stagnation approach points to the split in the National Party and indicates the support by thirty per cent of Afrikaners for the political concepts of the Verwoerd era. It points to the Afrikaner-Broederbond which, from the angle of the exclusive apartheid model, still ferments like leaven within the Afrikaner community. It points to the *baasskap* mentality which characterises the so-called new initiatives on constitutional development. It points to the rigid morality applied to censorship, Sunday sport and community culture which lies like a dead hand on South Africa. Meanwhile apartheid is alive and well in education, in the laws on race classification, in group areas, mixed marriages and immorality across the colour bar.

The nation and its philosophy are still reflected in the church of the Afrikaners.

Because of these reasons, so the argument goes, it is a sham that the Afrikaners are in the process of moving towards change. There are individuals, small pressure groups and a handful of academics who want to break away but the barriers of Afrikaner tradition are impenetrable and the Afrikaner guardians have the might to declare those who want to breach the laager, anathema.

I will oppose these arguments in this book, not by denying charges of stagnation, because every nation has its pigheaded component, its verkramptes and irrational ideologues. The percentage of those entrenched against change is not relevant.

What *is* relevant is whether the leadership corps of a nation is moving towards the boundaries of an old philosophy on the road to a new philosophy with a desire to come to terms with reality, using a new set of principles and goals.

If this leadership corps makes a meaningful impact, manages to recruit a significant number of followers and commands ever-increasing powers to define directions, a transition from the old to the new is inevitable.

If there is a new spirit abroad in the institutions of a nation, and if the seeds that have been sown germinate simultaneously on many levels, the harvest must follow, even if it takes a decade.

This is precisely what is happening in the Afrikaner community, probably something between revolution and reformation, which is why the (r)evolution of the title of this book implies both.

Revolution is total change with radical inputs destroying the old and creating the new. Reformation gives the existing order a newer and better appearance by adjustments, planing, omissions and shifts in accent. The popular distinction is that revolution is a new creation while reformation is restoration.

Reformation is a safer concept – that is why Afrikaner politicians choose the word – because it does not suggest wiping out the past. And revolution has gained a negative connotation in South Africa, implying revolt against order and the destruction of civilised norms.

I want to demonstrate that Afrikaner-evolution and Afrikaner-reformation possess the constructive energy to evolve into revolution. For decades Afrikaners have been part of, and have taken part in, a process of change in virtually all spheres. This process has not been completed, and never will be, because throughout the seasons of men and nations there are continuous shifts.

Every revolution has built-in evolution because change does not fall out of the sky. No revolution cuts all ties with the past. Rather, it is a process which strongly promotes certain ideas and denigrates others until the new ideas become embedded in new structures, policies and public opinion.

The energy for change is not equally distributed on all levels because (r)evolutions also occur in phases. Nor are these always conscious processes or even visible ones. It could best be described as a contagious atmosphere in which, through a chain reaction of events, words and decisions, human perspective is moulded and directed.

According to W A de Klerk in his book *The Puritans in Africa* the Afrikaner has already completed a revolution in the radical politics of apartheid from the late forties until the end of 1960.[1] As in all revolutions they used the battlecries of justice, calling, freedom and a utopian dream to restructure South African society into ethnically divided communities, legally placed into compartments and rigidly carried through on all levels. This revolution was carried by a kind of metaphysical messianism which became part of the Afrikaner's experience of self, of others, of the church of God. It permeated his system of principles and became a leitmotiv.

This book deals with the second (r)evolution of the Afrikaner which I want to typify as the break with the classic apartheid syndrome in politics, the church and community life to create a new concept of communality, making it the leitmotiv against apartheid. This new concept is still in a transitional phase but the urge towards change is unmistakable.

I use (r)evolution as a concept to describe the in between state of not yet revolution and no longer pure evolution.

The basic profile of Afrikaner philosophy is clearly recognisable in both (r)evolution and change.

These dynamics of the late seventies, which are gaining momentum and could reach a total breakthrough within six years, make the present period one of the most fascinating in South African history.

The links are the (r)evolution of political attitudes which relate to various basic changes, changing to the (r)evolution of political policy making. However, there is also a (r)evolution of religious convictions and the Afrikaans press has played a very important role in this (r)evolution.

Inevitably there will be repetition in this book because, with the focus on the Afrikaner, one looks at the same issue from different angles and details of one aspect will impinge when other aspects are discussed. A change in attitudes is a complex phenomenon interwoven with intricate dynamics. In analysing it one constantly rediscovers the same basic motivs.

Research, contemporary history or an empirical analysis of data form no part of this book. It is the work of a political journalist who, through the formulation of generalities, is attempting to present a perspective on the Afrikaner reality of today.

---

[1] De Klerk, W A. *The Puritans in Africa*. Harmondsworth: Penguin Books in association with Rex Collings, 1976.

1 The (R)evolution of Political Attitudes

1. From Uniformity to Pluriformity

Every human being and every nation has a self-image, often an idealised one. One of the aspects of such an image is that it describes stereotypes, in that the general characteristics of a nation are held to be true of its individual components.

The negative stereotype of the Afrikaner, created early in his history and built up over the past three decades, is the image of the malevolent Boer.

British travellers during the earliest British reign, missionaries before and during the Great Trek, and the British press during the Anglo-Boer War (1899–1902) built up a caricature of the Afrikaners as a self-contained group, essentially primitive, obdurate, heavily conservative and slow to think and act. They were described as a closed community, a second-rate and backward Dutch tribe in Africa who, in their isolation, rationalised their prestige by feelings of superiority over blacks because they were God's chosen. This gave them an arrogance which in practice came down to racist chauvinism callously striving for dominance.

In later years this stereotype was formulated in more civilised and hypocritical terms. It still implies, however, that the Afrikaners as a group maintain themselves by, and benefit from, a pitiless system of apartheid suppression and that more or less all Afrikaners perceive reality blinkered by this ideology.

Despite other voices in earlier and later writings of foreigners, despite the romantic European hero-worship of Boer bravery opposing British imperialism during the English War in 1899, despite sympathy for the tragedy of a small white nation in the black sea of Africa – the stereotype remains. Not only abroad but among many English-speakers in South Africa there is the belief that the Afrikaners are some kind of clan, conducting a refined reign of terror in South Africa.

This negative image has a complex background on which I do not propose to elaborate. One element is prejudice and malice. There is also a symbolic projection in which the Afrikaner is blamed for everything that goes wrong in South Africa. This symbolic projection can be extended: the Afrikaner is seen as an anachronism on an African continent, a colonial remnant attempting to subvert freedom, stability and democracy. All revolutionary movements need a negative stimulus. For black radicals the Afrikaners provide such a stimulus.

The negative image has also grown out of a misconception and incomprehension of the historical framework of Afrikaner history.

It is also true that there are Afrikaners who project these images. It would be grossly untrue to maintain that many Afrikaners are free of the stigma of racism, chauvinism, lack of culture and other repellent attitudes. However, all nations on earth house sub-groups one would prefer not to recognise.

The positive stereotype of the Afrikaner has been endlessly catalogued over the years by the nation's demagogues and also by many intellectual leaders.

An extract taken from these paeans of praise would read something like this: the Afrikaner is deeply religious; bound to the land; fired by a self-sacrificing nationalism; guided by high ethical norms of behaviour; has strong family ties; is both strict and just; is of high descent, born of Protestant Dutch and Huguenot stock; is motivated by freedom and traditional culture; and over and above all this, possesses the charming attributes of being friendly, helpful and hardworking.

This ideal is naive and wishful thinking. It's a generalised model of pretentious piety. In any case, all these 'attributes' can be found, individually and collectively, in other nations.

The mistake which is made both in and outside the country is in seeing the Afrikaners as a uniform group.

Naturally there were, and are, uniform tendencies among Afrikaners, as among all nations. Something like a national character does exist, although it is a woolly concept. Still, through a communal outlook on life and the world, a public opinion and a lifestyle are created to be transmitted by education and the process of identification.

The specific history of a nation is also a factor in creating a national character. The communal destiny of the archetypal Afrikaner, the frontier farmers, later the Voortrekkers, the added trauma of British imperial domination, all branded the Afrikaner character with the experience of threat and injustice.

The isolation, over many decades, from the sphere of influence of world culture, the vastness of the country, the small population, and the rural existence with its typical cultural content gave the Afrikaner a shuttered dimension.

His historical experience of the black man as an enemy created a prejudice which still exists today. In addition isolation emphasised their own 'threatened species' – the Afrikaners – which brought to Afrikaner tradition a tendency to exclusivity. Subjugated by the English, the pain he had to endure (and even today still endures in some places) of the contempt for his people by many English-speakers, strengthened the herd instinct and established suspicion and caution as lifestyles.

Calvinism also left its mark. Authority, law, principles, calling, freedom, a strong adherence to church and the pious norm in every area of life are typical Calvinist characteristics, part and parcel of the Afrikaner's awareness of what he should be. Therefore there were, and are, uniform characteristics among Afrikaners.

However, the quality of a disciplined national unit as a power factor for self-determination is a myth.

Uniformity has never meant political solidarity. Afrikaners have a tradition of dissent and disunity, which again proves that they are a 'normal' nation.

In the nineties of the eighteenth century there was bitter dissension in the Cape between the 'National Patriots' and the adherents of the House of Orange. This came about as a result of the French Revolution and led to the short-lived 'republics' of Graaff-Reinet and Swellendam.

The Great Trek has many important examples of dissension, especially among the supporters of the Trek leaders, Maritz, Potgieter and Retief. Typically, differences arose over constitutional action and over directions the Trek should take.

A deeper disunity which grew out of the Trek situation was that which emerged between the Transvalers and the Freestaters. In 1857 the Transvalers even mounted a commando raid into the Free State. The efforts of Marthinus Wessel Pretorius to unite the two republics were a dismal failure, while in the war of 1881 the Free State gave the Transvalers no formal aid.

The last years of the nineteenth century saw bitter infighting between Kruger supporters and those of Joubert.

It was in the present century, however, when the concept of an Afrikaner nation was already firmly established, that the worst dissension occurred. In 1912, shortly after Union, when the Afrikaners had been united under the old South African Party, they started splitting into two groups, Nat and Sap. Afrikaner shot at Afrikaner in the Rebellion of 1915. While the Nat/Sap division continued, coalition in 1934 added to the discord among Nationalist Afrikaners. There was the Gesuiwerde (Purified) National Party, later the Herenigde (Re-Unified) National Party, the Hertzogites in the newly-formed United Party and the Smuts men, also in the United Party. The year 1934 also saw the founding of the Ossewa-Brandwag which, during the war years, added more fuel to the fires of dissent, and it was also during the war that the old Hertzogites founded their Afrikaner Party.

Obviously dissent is the salient characteristic of our Afrikaans political history and, while it may have great disadvantages with regard to the Afrikaner's power base, it does serve a purpose in terms of the occasional national discussions so essential for establishing a new direction for the nation.

Today there are still undercurrents in Afrikanerdom. At present the dynamic of Afrikaner politics is a gauging process to find a way in which the South African realities can be handled.

The (r)evolution of the past decade or so sees the Afrikaner breaking away from a relative uniformity to pluriformity. The nation is breaching the walls of its own definitions.

No longer is the Afrikaner necessarily Calvinist. The influences of humanism, liberalism, methodism and pietism running through his experience give the lie to the image of the Calvinist Afrikaner. The unprecedented growth of the Pentecostal movement among Afrikaners, the indifference to the church, and agnosticism, are far cries from the Calvinist emphasis. Consciously active Calvinist Afrikaners are in fact in the minority.

The description of the Afrikaner as 'bound to his culture' is no longer valid. The Afrikaner has been absorbed into the modern city culture, right from his grassroots to the middle and upper classes. Exposed to a multiplicity of convictions, trends and values, he is in the process of undergoing a culture change which is bringing with it major shifts in thinking patterns, lifestyle and outlook on life. Physical, social and mental contact with the English-speaking element is increasing to such a degree that a broad South African identity is developing among the whites, alongside the typical Afrikaner cultural experience. The growing irritation among many Afrikaners with analyses and dictates about Afrikaner identity is a sure sign of impatience with exclusive role models of Afrikanership.

Nowadays the image of the politically self-contained Afrikaner doesn't hold water either, and it probably never will again. The National Party is no longer an Afrikaner front. Afrikaners are scattered among the Progressive Federal Party, the National Party, the Conservative Party and the Herstigte Nasionale Party.

The conformist mould has been broken. The so-called group discipline in which, from whatever leader, a 'shut up we know what's good for you' response is demanded, is now regarded with cynicism in many Afrikaans circles. Afrikaners are developing into a community in protest against many of the things which for years were accepted without question.

The concept of verligte and verkrampte Afrikaners has been accepted as part and parcel of their outlook on life. There are other differences: there is the stereotype Afrikaner with the laager mentality who finds his home in a monistic culture and group identification; there is the compromise Afrikaner who pragmatically widens the base of his identity; there is the liberal Afrikaner who has broken away from 'the truths of the nation'; and there is the Afrikaner who has come of age and no longer adheres to 'a past identity' and who rejects 'pre-cooked and pre-packaged' answers.[1]

Professor J J Degenaar intercedes for what he calls the morally critical Afrikaner as opposed to the nationalistic Afrikaner.[2] This concept, of the morally critical Afrikaner, gained support from some intellectual leaders and students. These Afrikaners do not wish to accept the nationalistic concept as their point of departure but rather a cultural concept, free of ethnicity, on which a new nation can be built with a common South African nationality, in which colour and race play no part.

Isolation and insularity have been breached and complete participation in the lifestyle of the twentieth century is now part of the Afrikaner experience. In this respect Afrikaner achievements in many fields have been remarkable, both in the quality of their leadership and entrepreneurial style. Industrial leaders, scientists, researchers, artists and professional men bear witness that the Afrikaners are bold leaders in a developing country.

The (r)evolution from a relative uniformity to a variegated pluriformity has broken the exclusive model of Afrikanership.

In the same way Afrikaner pride, the arrogance of appropriation and self-important pocketing all are dying attitudes. The 'otherness' in which at one time the Afrikaner sought to justify and entrench himself is making way for an awareness of the communal.

In my point of view Afrikaner identity is a hard won right which must be maintained. A sort of denial of self is naive. The Afrikaners as a group dare not diminish to a small minority which makes its cultural contribution by giving up its political power bases. In a pluriform country the Afrikaner also has a political identity, apart from his cultural one. The (r)evolution to accessibility, cultural cross-pollination and communality, and the breaking down of separateness and otherness is a positive energy. This (r)evolution saves the Afrikaner from diminishing to a clique, a kind of mystical something, both self-elevating and repulsive.

If we adhere to the old uniformity we will become obsolete.

The (r)evolution means that the Afrikaner is a nation-in-transition to a new identity, while retaining features of the old identity.

2. From Isolation to Communication

The discarding of isolation is a result of the current on-going process and deserves special attention. Afrikaner history has many examples of typical isolationist tendencies. The Great Trek (however acceptable the reasons for it), the belief of being a chosen people (however one-sidedly some observers of Afrikaners may stress this aspect), the dogma of apartheid (however one-sided or justifiable its presentation) and the minority group syndrome, in numbers and originally in influence (however subconsciously the psychology of this is executed) are examples of the isolationist dynamics which have affected the Afrikaner.

Within the historical context this isolationist attitude is understandable.

Inevitably, it brought self-centredness to the Afrikaner. He has a tradition which seeks the pivotal and which has turned self-assertion into a passion. Self-analysis and a preoccupation with being Afrikaans led to a form of narcissism and self-obsession. Everything that he perceived as a threat to the Afrikaner he kept outside the laager.

This narcissistic isolation became a barrier against English-speaking South Africans, against blacks and Coloureds, and against foreign political meddling in South African affairs.

Only if those outside the laager were useful to Afrikaner interests or agreed with Afrikaner philosophy were such outsiders partly accepted and tolerated.

In *The Super-Afrikaners* there is an extract from an Afrikaner-Broederbond document which illustrates this attitude.[3] The argument, according to the authors, is that the English-speakers are not really a nation in South Africa. The Afrikaners are the only white nation in the true sense of the word. Therefore the English-speakers must be 'afrikanerised' and Afrikaners must beware of becoming alienated from their roots through anglicisation.

The alienation of English-speakers, or conversely, the repudiation of the Afrikaner and his language by them, played a major role in Afrikaner history. After the Republic was established in 1961 the concept of co-operation became acceptable but on virtually all levels the distance was maintained.

Towards the Coloureds, Indians and blacks the Afrikaner traditionally maintained an attitude of total separation. This separation has diverse backgrounds. Philosophically the Afrikaner was steeped in such concepts as diversity, ethnicity, differentiation, separation and separateness. The difference in norms of civilisation and development served to widen the gap. The master-servant relationship was paternalistic, reflecting many humanitarian principles from care, aid and justice to bringing the message of Christianity. But the distance was maintained in social intercourse, in church worship and inter-personal relationships.

This distancing contained a definite element of self-aggrandisement but not of blatant racism. It was seen as part of the divine order which may not be disturbed. Examples of ironic inconsequences are myriad: the servant who handles the family's food and clothing; the baby and toddler at home in the arms of a black woman; black and white children who play and grow up together on farms. Still the distance was maintained, the boss mentality, the avoidance of any real contact. Apartheid merely entrenched this attitude in laws. It certainly wasn't created by the apartheid policy. As a result of apartheid institutions and the huge urbanisation process, a very real alienation occurred between Afrikaner and Coloured and black. Contact situations between black and white children – a characteristic of the rural tradition – virtually disappeared completely in the cities. Involvement in the lives of fellow beings became attenuated as the living-in servant remained a stranger in contrast to the black families on the farms who were an integral part of farm life. All that was left were the official, less personal relationships in the work situation.

With time this isolation created a chasm between the worlds of the Afrikaner and the black man. In fact, contact between black and white was officially sanctioned only on high levels; the lower down the scale one went, the less contact there was, especially in political matters and actualities of day to day living. Sport followed the same pattern. Only the top national teams were allowed to compete and for children all sporting contact was prohibited, justified by educational rationalisations.

Not that the Afrikaner ignored the blacks. The policy of apartheid tried to find a moral basis in the injunction of giving unto others that which you grant yourself. In most cases this meant the crumbs from the rich man's table, however much like sharing this may have seemed.

The attitudes of self-centredness and isolation are basic to the whole apartheid policy. With the Afrikaner as pivot, all other nations around him were fenced off; they were given their daily bread and they had to accept that the Afrikaner plan had their welfare, prosperity and identity in mind. Where blacks expressed doubts about the plan, both doubts and protest were rejected with an attitude of superior knowledge or indignation.

I am convinced that the Afrikaner sincerely believed

that what he was doing was right and proper, that he was leading the blind and smoothing the path of the 'black children' to a proud national existence, entirely separate from the pivot on which everything hinged – the Afrikaner nation, its rights, its philosophy and its extension.

This rationale was also applied to the Coloureds. The Indians were regarded as totally unwanted foreigners with no claims at all. The pot-pourri of English-speakers – British, Germans, Portuguese, Jews, Greeks – were seen as a complementary power base but only in so far as they respected the great Afrikaner plan for South Africa. The words of the Afrikaans writer C J Langenhoven are particularly apt: 'If you don't want to help me, don't hinder me.'

The basic attitude sketched above reveals a complacency, a sense of inviolability and arrogance, of narcissistic self-aggrandisement which would independently create the future, in the face of all opposition.

Foreign pressure elicited the same reaction from the average Afrikaner, from a kind of delusion of inviolability, strengthened by our mineral wealth and strategic situation, to an aggressive attitude of 'we can go it alone if they keep on at us'.

The (r)evolution that is taking place is the reversal of isolation to communication.

There are any number of explanations for the switch to communication. It is claimed that it is merely a strategy to involve outsiders through persuasion in the Afrikaner cause. It's the force of circumstance, say others, choosing communication out of fear for the loss of a power base. Therefore it must not be trusted.

I believe that it is a profound change in attitude and that at the core of it lies the Afrikaners' growing awareness that they cannot go it alone. It is a shift which is turning the traditional concept of 'Afrikanerness' upside down. The knowledge that he cannot stand alone means giving up exclusive thinking and accepting inclusive thinking; it means rejecting isolation and opting for openness and association; it means victory over the narcissistic self and an honest search for the other; it means a centrifugal energy which will see the realisation of self only in the communality of all in South Africa.

It is the rejection of separateness to make way for the communal. The accent is shifting from separation to cohesion, from apartheid to collectivity. More and more, arrogance must make way for humility, superiority for a healthy sense of dependency. The monologue-style is being replaced by the dialogue-style of deliberation on all levels. Deliberation means consultation, honest examination of the needs of other peoples, negotiation, interaction, participation and a joint say.

This (r)evolution is making the Afrikaner more receptive to the interests of others which in turn means the coming together and the discovering of other groups as neighbours, as allies and as fellow men, whose destinies are inseparably bound to that of the Afrikaner.

It is the (r)evolution of broadening of the concept of what it means to be an Afrikaner and the discovery of communality as the key to the future, set against the insularity of going it alone. The Afrikaners' attitude of accommodation is a dismantling of old concepts and a breakthrough to a new philosophy.

Communication is also aggressive, and for that reason the Afrikaner still rejects foreign meddling and prescriptions, the double standards applied to South Africa and the continued threats to and negation of new initiatives. The weak-kneed policy of the West which allows the dramatic growth of communism in our sub-continent must still be condemned. That is why the Afrikaner rules with a strong hand and strikes across our borders where terrorists are housed.

However, through this (r)evolution towards communication the Afrikaner has learned that in his isolation he must not think or do stupid things.

South Africa has an 'open' economy. A large part of our national wealth is derived from trade with other countries. The West has the power to do us considerable damage and if our economy is affected we will become increasingly politically defenceless. If we should be isolated from the West all the peoples of South Africa would be thrown into disarray, turning on one another like wolves. We are caught in the net of international conflicts from which we cannot escape. A stupid, hardnosed attitude could land us in a position where the interests of the West will demand our surrender. We would find ourselves dragged into the maelstrom and in the long run we shall drown. It is simply not a paying proposition to defy the West unnecessarily with stupidities. Every great era in history has its own mood which no one can evade. The present mood of the world encompasses social justice, non-discrimination, non-racist policies and equal opportunities for all.

The Afrikaner has arrived at an acceptance of these facts. With the utmost diplomacy, skill, integrity and horse trading, with sound parleying, initiative, negotiation and considered compromise, he is keeping the channels of communication open, both at home and in the international arena.

3. From Teuton to African

The Afrikaner is both alien and indigene in Africa.

The Afrikaans background, culture, traditions and way of life are still umbilically attached to Europe. Even if the Afrikaner nation is an independent off-shoot of the Dutch-German-French-English genealogical tree, that tree still provides nourishment.

Very early on in his history the Afrikaner showed that he did not have a typical colonial mentality but was taking on indigenous qualities. From as early as 1685 the language started to deviate from Dutch and by 1707 the term 'Afrikaner' was already in use. At the beginning of the nineteenth century the Afrikaners had a spiritual unity but the Great Trek and the Anglo-Boer War of 1899 gave substance to the awareness of being a nation.

A sort of ambivalence remained, however, which found expression in different attitudes, showing an unwillingness, as white Africans, to share a common destiny with black Africa.

The Afrikaner strictly maintained a traditional colour bar, raised discrimination to a right and paternally established the master/servant relationship.

The question is whether the typical traditional Afrikaner attitude is, at heart, racist?

Various explanations have been offered: the attitude results from Calvinist dogma; it is rooted in arrogance and fear; differences in civilised norms, which until recently were and even now are strongly marked, drew the colour line; the Afrikaner mobilised on an ethnic basis to gain and retain power as a minority group.

Probably all these statements contain a measure of truth but when one is exaggerated and held up as the basic motive distortion results. There is a definite racial dimension because black and white do threaten one another. There has been conflict between Afrikaners and Africans since the time of the border farmers in the Cape. Confrontation between individuals and groups, friction, clashing traditions, the chasm between civilisation and non-civilisation, and all the concomitant issues are part and parcel of the history of South Africa.

The experience of race and colour, especially when it is politicised, contains so many connotations, so much suppressed emotion and is so inflammable that the dream of a conflict-free South Africa is an idle one.

In the meantime black racism has gained enormous momentum, so much so that it is a universal phenomenon.

Against the background of black domination and black racist eruptions, notably in Zimbabwe, it must be accepted that racial conflict in South Africa will intensify, become total and progressively more emotional.

Despite all this — the traditional racist ballast and the present blazing evidence of black racism — the (r)evolution among Afrikaners to become Africans continues.

The Afrikaners are becoming more and more involved in, and are associating themselves with, Southern Africa, in the awareness that they are of Africa.

Neo-colonial attitudes of guardianship are being replaced by partnership, and paternalism by deliberations on an equal footing.

The Afrikaners are divesting themselves of colour obstructions. Colour isolation as a withdrawal from contact with blacks is making way for colour communication and mixing on social, sporting and professional levels. Colour barriers entrenched by discriminatory laws are being dismantled by Afrikaners – officially by the Afrikaner Government, but also under great pressure from Afrikaner intellectuals and certain church leaders. This is the (r)evolution of the Afrikaner making himself acceptable to Africa.

Colour fear, in its lack of trust and belief that agreement is impossible and that confrontation will be the only outcome, is being suppressed more and more in the wake of a new enthusiasm for co-existence.

It is the (r)evolution of moving away from racist prejudice and bulwarks to the identification with African aspirations and problems.

Concepts like justice and equality are taking on new content and application among Afrikaners.

Of course there are still many strongly-held attitudes, incidents and laws which are racially based but the voices of protest in the Afrikaner community and the Afrikaans press bear witness to an impatience with this tradition.

This (r)evolution, however, is not aimed at the denial of the ethnic reality of the existence of nations, nor is it a denial of the maintenance of the Afrikaner nation and its power base.

The (r)evolution could lead to a shifting of border posts, expanding Afrikaner identity to include those who associate themselves with the Afrikaner group, with his language and aspirations, for example those Coloureds and Europeans who identify with the Afrikaner.

It would be devolution to expose a nation to dissolution, self-destruction and assimilation. Giving up a hard-gained position of leadership goes against the human grain, politically and historically.

The (r)evolution rather implies the defusion of ethnicity as a factor of separation, to an ethnicity which, apart from the acceptance of one's own, can also accept others as part of the South African family which, without barriers, can build a broad nationalism.

The (r)evolution will gain further momentum if the Afrikaner were accepted by the blacks, that is an acceptance of his indigenity, his history, the (r)evolution in his attitudes and the offer of his new dispensation.

Unlike the white experience of blacks, South African blacks will have to prove that they are not going to allow themselves to be carried away by racist hate in an anti-white passion. The blacks must learn from the African experience that at this moment in time their capacity for government is not well-developed; their governments too often degenerate into mere power political struggles. They are inexperienced in administration, organisation and management. Their productivity, initiative and sustained continuity of enterprise are limited.

My intention is not to be offensive but to state these things as factual information so that blacks in South Africa can also strive for a level-headed approach.

The blacks must keep their eyes and ears open regarding conditions on the rest of the continent and try for a better understanding of the fact that development aid in South Africa has up to now achieved more than almost the rest of Africa put together. They will also have to undergo another (r)evolution and that is to accept the partnership with the white man in South Africa with more enthusiasm.

The whites (Afrikaners) must realise that our economy, our standard of living, our peace and prosperity will be determined by the success of our guidance, by the scope and intensity of black education and educational programmes, and by the measure in which the black man's sense of self-respect is strengthened.

4. From Insecurity to Security

In his history the Afrikaner has without doubt had to work through a great load of insecurities.

The threats against him were perceived as the main causes of insecurity: the English colonialists, the attacks of the blacks on his safety and possessions and the historic fear of being ploughed under. Even today there is the threat of the Communist onslaught on Southern Africa, the threat of black racism and imperialism and the aggressive attitude of the West.

Over the years economic insecurity also took its toll. The ruins after the Anglo-Boer War, the great droughts, the descent into poverty and, initially, the anonymity and trauma in the move to the cities, left their stamp.

Many Afrikaners would deny it, but it was this stamp of insecurity which created the inferiority syndrome. There were few resources on which to fall back because the nation was scattered, small in numbers, young and defenceless.

Out of these insecurities of threat, homelessness, inferiority and feelings of humiliation, a negative nationalism was born. The English were the biggest source of offence and they gave plenty of cause. The Afrikaner became over-sensitive to criticism, closed to non-Afrikaners and suspicious of being undermined on all fronts.

In the past few years there has been a (r)evolution from negative Afrikaner nationalism to positive nationalism. A (r)evolution from an infantile insecurity with everything that results from such insecurity to a self-assurance on a more adult level. Signs of this (r)evolution to maturity are: a critical sense, even within their own ranks, the candour with which Afrikaners state their differences and points of view in the public debate, the capacity to view themselves and their problems from a distance and the moral courage to make choices.

The passion for excommunication which casts 'heretics' out of the Afrikaner corps has been tempered, especially in intellectual and professional Afrikaner circles.

That there are still many Afrikaners who, with their vehement emotionalism and immature certainties, lack political sophistication, does not detract from the momentum of the (r)evolution to self-assurance.

The Afrikaner is acquiring an established feeling of identity which makes him less desperate when facing threats. He is more readily playing a leading role in Africa, with a realisation of his responsibility towards the politics of accommodation.

5. From Acceptance to Examination

Historically the Afrikaner nation, its authors and its leaders have never been critical of the image, motivations, attitudes and aims of the Afrikaner.

The historian F A van Jaarsveld found, after extensive research, that the Afrikaner has written very little about himself.[4] He refers to a statement made by Dr Gerrit Viljoen (now a cabinet minister) in which he alleged that the Afrikaner loves to talk about himself but refuses to look at himself critically and that the reason for this lies in a lack of self-assurance and an aversion to the outside criticism to which Afrikaners are exposed.

The great emphasis on national unity from the thirties to the fifties and later established this uncritical acceptance of the vision of Afrikaner leaders. After the National Party came to power in 1948 a kind of indoctrination of the Afrikaner ideal of apartheid led to a conformism which blunted the critical faculty. Any deviation from the designed model of the Afrikaner's political approach was feared because excommunication from the circle of true Afrikaners, a fate worse than death, befell those individuals who resisted the 'will of the nation' as formulated by politicians, church and cultural leaders. Loyalty to acknowledged leaders was projected as the characteristic of purity. The Afrikaners were conditioned to believe that the policy of apartheid would be a solution and they were constantly reassured on this score. Perhaps it was wishful thinking but their belief in this policy was overwhelming.

There were, however, many voices crying in the wilderness: some academics, the newer generation of Afrikaans writers, the Sestigers, with their 'literature of involvement', and a few Afrikaans newspapers who early on in the seventies started sounding the alarm that the apartheid model was not capable of solving all the country's problems. Apart from adjustments in policy, the politicians continued to decry the standpoints in Afrikaans newspapers and lauded apartheid as the only truth.

During this period the 'verligte movement' among Afrikaners was branded as liberalism. The verligtes who openly dared to take a stand were thin on the ground and if the pressure from politicians became too intense it was not unusual for them to change course in order to save their own skins.

Apart from these verligte warning bells calling Afrikaners to account, three events started the (r)evolution.

The riots which erupted in Soweto and other black urban areas in 1976 destroyed the dream that blacks tolerated apartheid, that it was only a question of time before they tasted the fruits of utopia and were converted. The bitterness of the urban black and his grievances shook thinking Afrikaners to the core.

During 1978 the Information Scandal bred Afrikaner scepticism about the trustworthiness of his top leaders. Corrupt power, lies and deceit, crooked means to justify the end, over-protection of people, mistaken loyalties, a cover-up of the true facts ... all these practices caused a major scandal.

The spirit of examination, criticism and disillusion gained great momentum in Afrikaans circles. The attitude of not swallowing everything one is told in politics and that a blind loyalty to leaders is dangerous, rapidly gained ground.

Shortly after P W Botha came to power as prime minister in 1978 he shook the old belief in apartheid when he revealed himself as a verligte by openly stating that radical changes had to be made.

For many Afrikaners this was too much to digest. With disillusionment came all the familiar accompanying phenomena: protest, intolerance, irritation, a falling back on the familiar and a witch-hunt of the so-called 'sell outs'.

This led to the political split which will be dealt with in a later chapter.

The irritation also increased in the verligte camp. In newspapers, publications, symposia and speeches the policy began to be questioned, boldly and publicly.

The (r)evolution from acceptance to examination, and the (r)evolution of self-justification to an Afrikaner awareness of guilt, was born.

This questioning was applied to virtually all areas.

Questioning those aspects already discussed in this chapter: the definitions of 'Afrikanership', the untenability of the South African isolation, the attachment to Africa and Afrikaner security and maturity.

Questioning the Afrikaner concept of self: is he the exclusive ruling group or the threatened minority who cannot go it alone? Isn't inter-dependence a bigger truth than independence? Has the ethnic not been over-emphasised?

Questioning the one-sidedness of the policy of apartheid which finds its leitmotiv in the homelands, underlining in particular the failure of homeland development and the problem of absorption of blacks who were supposed to go back to their homelands and border industries. Questioning labour demands in South Africa and the economic feasibility of the basic concepts of the policy. Questioning the political rights of the urban blacks and the senselessness of shunting them back to the homelands to exercise these rights. Questioning the absurdity of rigid divisions in sport and in other unnecessary areas. Questioning Coloured and Indian rights and citizenship. Questioning the statutory entrenchment of apartheid and structural discrimination. Questioning the whole moral basis of the concept of apartheid.

These examples of questioning are indisputable signs of (r)evolution in Afrikaner attitudes. The discovery that the apartheid tradition is too idealistic, too ideological, too regimented, too one-sided and too repellent are the first fruits of the (r)evolution.

This led from self-justification to a sense of guilt. Guilt, sacrifice and forgiveness go together.

First the guilt ....

In my honest opinion the white (Afrikaner) need feel no guilt about people of colour in the sense of deliberate malice and the plotting of evil towards them. From colonial times, and after, whites many times tried to come to terms with people of different colour by means of negotiation and discussion. Inter-personal relationships were always good. For generations whites gave constructive service in the interests of black and brown.

The policy of separate development was an attempt to

establish freedom, justice, self-expression and self-preservation and to reject domination.

The Afrikaner has also been forgiving because he too has been at the receiving end of a great deal of ill-will. Revenge, as distinct from retribution, never played a role.

And yet, there is a communal guilt which must be accepted and naturally non-whites must shoulder a load of guilt as well.

I want to list the burdens of guilt of the Afrikaner.

The guilt of lost opportunities. The development of the homelands might have been enthusiastically accepted by blacks if we had, at the time, moved mountains to deliver the goods; border industries, decentralisation and physical planning could have been an established pattern had we thought big; the alienation between us and the Coloureds could have been prevented had we drawn them nearer when they were still near us.

This list of lost chances, of wasting of opportunities, shortsightedness and lotus-eating can be stretched into infinity.

The guilt of greed. We too often wanted the cream off the top, wanted no further sharing. The minimum for Coloureds was the maxim.

The guilt of one-sidedness. Separateness grew like an untrained creeper so that communality was virtually strangled to death. Everything was pigeon-holed. In this manner we created a climate of rejection.

The guilt of colour isolation. It became our highest norm and we were seduced into a whole system of discrimination and destructive separation, with a kind of withdrawal from contact, discussion, deliberation and mutual influencing.

The guilt of arrogance.

This brings us to the sacrifice ...

What must we sacrifice to expiate our guilt? Not our identity; not abdication of our political authority; no sickly cap-in-hand atonement; no drawing of a line through our policy; no throwing overboard of colour barriers ... all these things, and more, are part of reality and of our right, which we demand without shame.

The sacrifice that is asked of us is to set aside the mentality of autocracy and the false barriers of injustice, arrogance and rejection in which we tried to take cover.

We will have to go forth in a spirit of reconciliation, erasing some of our tracks, and from the bottom of our hearts make a new beginning, building on what was positive in the past.

And the expiation?

Expiation will come when we can turn the four burdens of guilt into four initiatives.

Initiative to make use of our chances, to replace our greed with sharing, to overcome our one-sidedness with balance and to break through our colour isolation with orderly association.

This is exactly what reformation politics are all about. There are still open doors for a settlement among peoples in which the white man will be able to exercise his rights. There is still a possibility of establishing physical planning by decentralisation. Constitutionally the policy of self-determination and joint determination can still succeed between whites, Coloureds and Indians, and with blacks in a confederation. There is still enough understanding that differentiation is valid, if communality comes into its own; if the main differentiation is still acceptable, if discrimination disappears.

History will expiate the Afrikaner from his guilt of neglect if he offers proof – in attitude and deed – that he understands the demands of his era and that he is not fearfully hiding from the task which now rests on his shoulders.

If we do not do this this generation will be unable to look anyone in the eye. And our own guilt will devour us.

6. *From Problems to Solutions*

Traditionally the Afrikaners have always had three attitudes to their political problems, namely escapism, bravado and pessimism.

The problems which threaten our country are drowned in words, minimised and ignored: Many of our people simply refuse to face facts. It is this attitude which resolves nothing; it is rather a prelude to the great collapse.

The problems which threaten our country can be solved by force: Bravado has always been weakness. It is megalomania and a provocation of reality. It is stupid heroics or, even worse, loudmouthed cowardice.

The problems which threaten our country are overpowering us: This is the fall-of-the-empire state of mind which constantly undermines morale, the feeling that we in this country are pawns in the irrevocable game of history. We merely wait for the end, accepting things as they are and, if necessary, we will, like Samson, pull down the pillars on a generation predestined for the heroic-tragical. It is something akin to a death wish, which is defeating the hope of many of our people.

The attitude with which we face the future is of the utmost importance. It is a source of both energy and motivation.

With a crowd of blind men, make-or-break men and pessimists one simply cannot win.

The (r)evolution means that the Afrikaner is moving away from ideology to realism and practical politics. Afrikaners no longer blind themselves to the fact that we are a multi-national country, interwoven in all areas; that black expectations have a moral, defensible and logical basis; that the sheer number of blacks demands a solution which is also acceptable to them; that labour, economy and education demand a new dispensation which must irrevocably come.

A political policy must be both acceptable and feasible and aim at a disposition between nations.

It's the political attitude of the will to win.

It demands a cold and sober assessment of the problems as opposed to suppression of the facts of our situation.

It demands careful computation of all the choices, as against the storm troopers.

It demands the rejection of paralysis (to which the facts in South Africa can seduce one) and the death wish.

I have previously quoted the description of morale as 'that abiding feeling of strength and superiority which at the very outset gives an attitude of confidence and assurance of victory'.

I also wrote about it thus: awareness of threat + computation of your abilities + a realisation of urgency + clear aims and a strategy to realise them + an attitude of belief in your cause + tough, calm, methodical perseverance + trust in your national and philosophical power sources, are the building bricks of morale.

The Afrikaner is moving towards this mental attitude.

SUMMING UP

The energy fermenting among Afrikaners of the eighties must be correctly assessed.

It is the (r)evolution of a nation-in-transition to a new identity.

It is the (r)evolution from the isolation of self-aggrandisement to the knowledge that the Afrikaner cannot walk the road alone.

It is the (r)evolution of making himself acceptable to black Africa and the West, a moving away from racism and a defusing of ethnicity, to an identification with co-existence where the separation factor is not the dominant one.

It is the (r)evolution from infantile insecurity to self-assurance on a more positive and mature level.

It is the (r)evolution from acceptance of the apartheid system in all its detail to critical questioning.

It is the (r)evolution from self-accusation to a healthy national awareness of guilt.

It is the (r)evolution of moving from ideological to realistic politics.

The emphasis is shifting from exclusivity to inclusivity, from the centripetal energy to the centrifugal energy of common interests, from separation to cohesion, from apartheid to communality.

The motivation for the (r)evolution is fear for self-preservation but it also includes a new vision of self, of concepts like democracy, justice and equality.

This (r)evolution is not mere rhetoric and symbolic gestures, nor cosmetic change. It is a basic shift in emphasis which has already brought a new philosophy to some, which finds others still running away from the breakthrough, and many caught up in the dichotomy of doubt.

This (r)evolution is a tentative search for a change in political policies which will bring about an accommodation between nations in South Africa.

[1] Alant, C J. 'Die Profiel van 'n Afrikaner: 'n Sosiologiese Verkenning'. Inaugural address. University of South Africa, 2 March 1978.
[2] Degenaar, Prof J J. *Keuse vir die Afrikaner*. Johannesburg: Taurus Publishers, 1982.
[3] Wilkins, I and Strydom, H. *The Super-Afrikaners: Inside the Afrikaner-Broederbond*. Johannesburg: Jonathan Ball Publishers, 1978.
[4] Van Jaarsveld, F A. *Wie en Wat is die Afrikaner?* Cape Town: Tafelberg Publishers, 1981.

2 The (R)evolution of Political Policy

1. The Split in the National Party

The (r)evolution of political attitudes came to life through the deep divisions among Afrikaners on the political level.

The first split came in 1969 when the Herstigte Nasionale Party broke with Prime Minister John Vorster and the second came with the formation of the Conservative Party under the leadership of Dr A P Treurnicht in 1982. These two groups have the same philosophy and will therefore not be discussed separately.

The division was not a 'clean break' between progressive and conservative; at the root of the split was a mixture of motives. Provincialism in South Africa played a role – Conservative Party supporters take pride in seeing themselves as the purified Nationalists of the Transvaal, who are unable to accommodate the Cape liberal Nationalists. Old personal vendettas and suspicions played a part too: Dr Treurnicht has been distrusted by some members within the NP since the HNP was founded, and his controversial statements made time and time again on the interpretation of policy by Prime Minister P W Botha fed the distrust.

Frustration, ambition, revenge and other emotions are always present in political rows.

The most generally accepted explanation of the split was, and still is, that it had to do with personalities and the interpretation of details, not about real differences of principle.

This is a superficial explanation. Now that the divisions have come out into the open it is possible to see the differences between philosophical and personal motives. As a result of this, the Afrikaners' political divisions will evince

themselves in two different political approaches.
Years before the split, the author, in a newspaper article, forecast it as a split on principles. The article argued that a group of Afrikaners would break away from the National Party over four issues: one Parliament for Coloureds, Asians and whites; the establishment of a firm confederation in which both urban blacks and the black national states would be involved; the abolition of separation laws; and racially mixed state authorities.
Precisely these principles were at the heart of the split.
The split was about inclusive thinking (Afrikaners cannot go it alone politically and must therefore share power), set against exclusive political thinking (the self-preservation of the Afrikaner is dependent on a barrier between his political and community life and that of other population groups). The polarisation is communality as opposed to separateness; reciprocal interaction as opposed to apartheid.
The basic philosophy of the Conservative Party is apartheid with the widest possible separation, enforced on all levels, its central motive the maintenance of the Afrikaner nation's identity as the pivotal nation.
To make this possible they chose three policy directions: territorial separation, white supremacy and extensive unravelling of black and white.
Territorial separation means that they will have a great many things to tackle at one and the same time. All black areas will have to be consolidated into four main blocks by exchanging land. A number of areas will be proclaimed for Coloureds and Indians and what is left will be white South Africa under Afrikaner rule.
By moving the boundaries of the homelands, certain black suburbs will be incorporated into the homelands and blacks will be transplanted from the white country to black cities in homelands from where express transport systems will take them to and from their work in white areas. The blacks inevitably remaining in white areas will be guest labourers entitled to limited local government under the guidance of white authorities.
White supremacy holds good for the Coloureds and

Indians because in their 'countries' they will have self-government but in the majority of communal affairs, affecting virtually everything, the white Parliament will have the only say. On regional and local government levels those in authority will be white. Later, perhaps, some form of loose confederation may develop between the white Republic and the Coloured cantons within its borders, but any mixed bodies on any government level are wholly unacceptable.

The political relationship between this white-controlled state and the black states is that of co-operation and a mutual exchange of services, but a permanent structure where communal issues can be discussed and decided upon is rejected. In actual fact, the communal on this inter-state level is also subject to white will.

The drastic unravelling must take place on three levels.

Colour-unravelling must occur because the full power of the colour bar must be maintained. Discriminatory measures are essential and where amenities are shared by the population groups this must be controlled by permits and then only by way of exception. The Immorality Act must be extended to immorality between all people, including black and brown. Sport must be separate, except on international level when national teams will compete. In the labour market there must be job reservation for whites, black trade unions must be banned and no mixed work situation will be allowed. Any mixed council, commission or institution will be disbanded and re-composed separately.

An unravelling of Afrikaners from the English and foreign investors must also take place because these economic masters undermine apartheid. An unravelling must take place to release South West Africa/Namibia from the United Nations and an apartheid solution will be applied there. The apartheid state will go its own way and will doubtless survive any boycotts.

This Conservative Party philosophy has been summed up to prove the argument that the split was the result of conflicting principles.

It also proves the following argument, namely that the

Conservative Party represents resistance to the Afrikaner (r)evolution. It may also be called the devolution-energy because it implies a relapse into the attitudes of isolation, self-aggrandisement, Afrikaner separateness, racism, narcissism and ideology. It is the typical continuation of the rejection-politics, confrontation-politics, isolation-politics and domination of a past era.

The fact that the majority of Afrikaners rejects this party – according to election results they have a conjectured 30 per cent of Afrikaner support – is a sign that the Afrikaner (r)evolution is also on the point of breaking through into the area of political policy.

Political groupings among Afrikaners are far from complete. Politically speaking, there are still many 'in-between Afrikaners' hesitating between devolution and evolution before they become part of the (r)evolution. When the new politics of the National Party have been tried and tested their drawing power among Afrikaners will increase because they will be overwhelmed by the (r)evolution of Afrikaner attitudes.

However, there is a very delicate balance. If the future in South Africa becomes more ungovernable and if the new politics of the Afrikaner is brought up short by its rejection by black and brown groups, a falling back may result in attempts to find self-protection in the old policy.

That is why it is of the utmost importance that the (r)evolution of political policy takes place in an orderly and evolutionary fashion. Within the National Party there are centrist groups, who merely want to polish the old policy, there are the confused, who sceptically follow the new initiatives, and there are the verligtes who are ripe for the new politics.

Between the (r)evolution of political attitudes and the (r)evolution of political policy lies a minefield that must be carefully negotiated.

In essence, however, the (r)evolution of political policy is present in the majority of Afrikaners and it is merely marking time before becoming a reality within the next decade.

2. The (R)evolution is Afrikaner Compromise-Politics

A thorough examination of the two political mainstreams in South Africa is essential for an understanding of the new politics of the Afrikaner. With the partial failure of one (the separate nations concept) and the rejection of the other (the unitarian state concept), the new compromise-politics was born. Therein lies the (r)evolution.

All politics in South Africa can be traced back to either the idea of a unitary state or the idea of nation states.

The unitary state concept claims that all the inhabitants of South Africa share a common nationality, that they therefore must vote on a common roll to choose one parliament so that all share in one and the same political process. The consequences are total political integration and the lapsing of all racial differences in South African politics.

This unitary state can have many forms – a classic Westminster unitary state with or without entrenched rights for minorities, or various federation models of territorial areas.

The Afrikaners reject this constitutional system, and continue to do so, despite pressure from black leaders, the Progressive Federal Party in South Africa and the Western powers.

The (r)evolution of political policy in the Afrikaans community will not willingly follow this course. If history forces it upon them the Afrikaners will submit under protest and in all probability, in the ensuing political conflict, be so ground down that little will remain of the profile of today's Afrikaner. The greatest fear is that this form of government will result in the elimination of the Afrikaner (and the whites) in many areas.

This fear is certainly not without ground.

The imbalance in numbers will cause the surrender of minorities; constitutions cannot succeed when they are built on the taking away of political power of minority groups and constitutional entrenchments are not worth the paper they're written on if they are not supported by power political structures. The historical experience in Africa is the subjection of minorities by the majority.

This unitary state will inevitably mean a black majority state. Against the background of the white/black conflict, the difference in numbers, standards, norms, possessions and culture between black and white, and the events in Zimbabwe, such a unitary state will result in irreconcilable politics which will be consumed by confrontation.

The black nations, especially their moderate leaders, also have reservations; they fear that in a unitary state subjugation under one or other black nation will result. That is Africa-style – once political power has been gained black solidarity quickly disappears to make room for the domination of one black group by another.

Afrikaners will therefore not be persuaded to accept a unitary state.

The reply of many to this Afrikaner refusal is that the unitary state will be forced upon them by a black revolution.

Afrikaners are aware of this threat but find their comfort in studies on the subject of revolution which state that revolution is only possible if there is a breakdown in the administration of the civil service and an infiltration of revolutionary action; if the revolutionary forces are, on all levels, a match for the opposing force; and if the revolutionary and other sources remain open for all the needs and necessary supplies.

Measured against these standards, South Africa is not an easy prey for a revolution. But the fear of revolution cannot be so easily put aside. International powers, subversion and terror, sabotage and instability can make South Africa ripe for black revolution.

The (r)evolution of Afrikaners to compromise-politics will not necessarily prevent a black revolution either. In his book *South Africa after Vorster* Arnheim writes in great detail about reactions to political development.[1] He says that the revolutionaries always keep in mind the inevitable success of the revolution; the moderates claim that a compromise formula is the only solution; and the reactionaries are convinced that a bloodbath can only be avoided by a return to apartheid.

Arnheim says that the blacks will demand more and

more and the government will concede more and more. However, this will not prevent the revolution because the more the black middle class emerges, the more political unrest and the more comprehensive the political change, the closer South Africa moves to radicalisation and revolution. His conclusion is that of the fatalist and historical determinist who says what will be will be. History marches to its own drumbeat and no matter what is devised for South Africa no peaceful and lasting solution can be found.

The (r)evolution of the Afrikaners' political policy will never break through to the idea of a unitary state. This (r)evolution is rooted rather in a growing awareness that black demands must be accommodated in a manner that is acceptable to blacks. Behind this growing awareness lies the fear of a black revolution.

Afrikaners are realising more and more that there is no permanent, satisfactory and ideal solution for South African politics, whatever that ideal might be seen from the side of the Afrikaner, the whites or the blacks.

The (r)evolution of comprehension that black and brown must have true freedom – the political freedom of joint say, freedom in the labour market with bargaining power, social freedom from any form of discrimination and individual freedom with regard to inalienable human rights.

The (r)evolution can also be called a (r)evolution of the relativisation of political options. The unitary state is rejected but there is an element of the unitary state which cannot be ignored in the South African political system. This (r)evolution of the relativisation of political options is also making Afrikaners realise that politics is a cycle of processes and not the completion of a preconceived concept.

The idea of an open-ended solution to the political processes is beginning to be accepted by Afrikaners, as is an awareness that in the continuation of the processes there will always be the rhythm of polarisation, conflict, confrontation and compromise. In such a political process, viewpoints are stated, corns are trodden on, there are reproaches, threats, insults, breakaways ... but there is also an acceptance of differences, new formulas, superficial reconciliations, co-operation in mutual self-interest ... until something happens to polarise each group in its own camp from where its power base can function.

Although the unitary state is rejected the (r)evolution of the relativisation of political options is taking root among Afrikaners and this is opening the way to compromise-politics.

The nation-state concepts?

These concepts have been badly eroded, a factor which also contributes to Afrikaner receptivity for compromise-politics.

The essence of the concepts is that there are identifiable nations in South Africa, each with its own history and territory. Seen in this light, there is no majority group in South Africa, only minority groups.

Each nation has the right to a nation-state and must accept the nationality of that state. In the case of whites, they are a conglomeration and are therefore seen as one nation which can form one state. It is easy to differentiate among the black nations, while the Coloureds are a nation in the making and the Indians are a minority group. For this reason a nation-state for every identifiable group is not feasible.

The basic concept is segregation, the division of political power and the maintenance of good neighbourliness by means of various co-operation models.

In practice, these concepts have become less and less feasible.

The development of the homelands has, for various reasons, not taken place in accordance with the dream. They were unable to absorb the blacks and the development of border industries was negligible. Consolidation of the homelands has not been an unqualified success due to high costs, conflict with farmers reluctant to part with their land and the insufficient utilisation of the land by blacks.

Developments within South Africa dictated by labour demands necessitated an influx of blacks into white areas. Forty-three per cent of blacks live and work outside their homelands, and by the year 2020 South Africa (the 'white' country) will have 31,4 million blacks in its midst.

The nation-state concept in its theoretical and idealised form has not become reality. Economic integration rejected it; the lack of viability and black resistance rejected it, even after the independence of some of the black states; the rise, settlement, development and agitation of urban blacks, and their alienation from their homelands, rejected it; the huge sums of money needed to make a success of the concept rejected it; the lack of independence, judgement, initiative and entrepreneurship of the blacks rejected it.

This ideological apartheid and its accompanying discrimination was seen as racist rejection. The policy became more and more morally suspect and the growing black nationalism and black power which demands equal possession of the Republic and power-sharing, became a tidal wave, battering against the barriers of apartheid.

For Afrikaners the concept has become less and less feasible because it is too idealistic, too ideological, too one-sided and too regimented.

The Afrikaner started to discover that his key word – ethnicity – gravely affronted even moderate Coloureds and blacks, and filled them with loathing.

Racial and national groups are acknowledged by blacks as part of reality. They can find no fault with nationalism and awareness of own culture and language. They understand ethnic groups as political power groups.

The non-revolutionary middle class blacks even foresee that separate national groups must rule themselves, working towards a common liaison.

But the point-blank rejection, the refusal to budge, is evoked by what they call forced ethnicity. By that they mean that Afrikaners want to force ethnicity on South Africa as a basic pattern and a divisive factor. It is the coercion of legally enforced racial groupings, across the whole spectrum of life, which is so obnoxious – politics, voters' rolls, state institutions, public amenities, education, living areas, marriage and a comprehensive list of other things.

They do not want group mixing but enforced group apartheid is unacceptable, however it might be explained.

It is against this wall of protest that Afrikaners are banging their heads. It is protest against the interference with personal liberty, with its right of a choice of association. It is protest founded on a background in which the whites reject the black race out of a sense of superiority. It is protest against the fact that for blacks ethnicity implies injustice, suppression, insult and blocked opportunities.

All the barriers mentioned have brought Afrikaners to the realisation that the concept of apartheid as a political policy is doomed to failure.

Two options were considered – either a dictatorship or radical separation.

Dictatorship, which enforces either verkrampte apartheid or verligte reformation politics – this the Afrikaner is also beginning to realise – will only magnify the country's problems because historically self-maintenance by means of power has never succeeded in the long run.

The other option discussed in Afrikaner circles is radical separation. Because white and black demands are, in all probability, irreconcilable, and because the disparity in numbers, cultural diversity and political conflict make a solution impossible, the idea of radical territorial separation was mooted.

There are different models for this idea: all the black homelands will be consolidated into four main blocks; the remainder will be white South Africa. The country's provinces are to be re-partitioned to excise the white provinces. A white-cum-Coloured separation must take place towards the south, cutting diagonally across the country (Sishen, Bloemfontein, Port Elizabeth), which will establish a white country south of the line, set against a black country north of the line.

The stumbling blocks in the way of such radical partition are myriad. How can millions of people be shifted and resettled? Quite apart from the resistance which would be encountered, the costs would be astronomical.

If the Transvaal became a black country the white economy would be irrevocably weakened and the whites would lose their political bargaining power, both within and outside the country. The northern black state would be open to infiltration by external powers, threatening the neighbourly relations of the white country. The white state would be hemmed in in the Karoo and the Boland.

Such a solution would be internationally unacceptable because white insistence on self-determination is not regarded sympathetically.

The extent of the territorial blending of races in South Africa makes radical separation impracticable.

The (r)evolution of the Afrikaners' political policy is rooted in the growing awareness that the separation policy, according to the traditional plan, offers no solution for South Africa.

It is a (r)evolution away from the nation-state concept of separation to the new politics of collectivity.

However, the dilemma remains that neither the unitary state concept, nor the nation-state ideal offers a solution.

That is why the Afrikaner is turning to compromise-politics, and this turning is a (r)evolution of political policy.

The philosophy of the new compromise-politics contains the following elements:

— the disposition of nations is the political ideal, not confrontation between nations or their subjugation.
— the disposition of nations cannot be attained through the concepts of a unitary state or separate nation-states.
— the dispensation of nations is only possible by creating a nation concept which contains elements of both a unitary state and nation-states. All parties must be persuaded to agree to this compromise dispensation.
— the compromise formula is authority over own affairs and shared authority for all the peoples and groups in South Africa. This is called the politics of association.
— the unitary state as concept is recognised in this compromise in the participation on all levels of government, full participation on the communal level by all and the abolition of legal discrimination. Ethnicity as an enforced social separation would be largely abolished, except where group interests were the decisive factor. There would be joint citizenship and the sharing of public amenities, wherever desirable.
— the nation-state concept is recognised in this com-

promise because ethnicity as a political division is retained, and territorial division as a political creed is abandoned. The point of departure is that population groups remain the basic bricks of politics and society and that group autonomy is retained by authority over own affairs. Own affairs can be decided in an on-going process of consultation, but basically this means that the sphere of existence of each group, their 'own' sphere, will be maintained by their own political structures, own living areas, education and establishments. However, the entrenchment of the own sphere also compromises by permitting a 'grey sphere' in living areas, education etcetera, where the right of choice to take part in the grey sphere will be acknowledged.

The Afrikaners have not completed the (r)evolution to compromise-politics. Apart from the rejection thereof by Afrikaners who support the Conservative Party and other rightwing groups, the National Party, which is in the midst of this (r)evolution, is not yet ready to execute the whole compromise. The new vision of ethnicity which, except as a political division, should not be enforced, is still unacceptable to many leaders and their followers.

However, the process of this (r)evolution is irreversible, not only as a result of outside pressures but also as a result of the (r)evolution of attitudes among Afrikaners.

The absolute condition for the success of compromise-politics, if the Afrikaners hope to achieve the goal, is the abandonment of many aspects of ethnicity as an enforceable social measure.

This (r)evolution is not merely a compromise for the sake of survival, but a (r)evolution away from a blindness to truth and reality, towards the light of a clear awareness of truth and reality.

This statement is based on a view of life in which truth and reality exist as two poles which often seem paradoxical. The completeness of an issue or a person cannot be captured in one formula but in dual conceptions which appear to be paradoxical. In the balance between the two poles reality and truth are threaded like the string on the two ends of a bow.

Applied to politics, the two poles of separateness and cohesion are the framework in which the truth of the South African reality may be grasped.

In South Africa separate nations are bound to a common destiny. The differences of colour, race, nationality and culture are fact, and the maintenance of such differences is the right of individual choice, but it also contains other dynamics which motivate self-preservation. The acknowledgement of communality, inter-dependence and intermingling demands, along with separateness, cohesion, interaction and the the structuring of collectivity.

The (r)evolution of political attitudes and political policies in the formula of own authority and shared authority is therefore not some kind of timid and unnatural compromise, but the (r)evolution to an enlightened vision of reality. It is a (r)evolution back to a clear awareness of, and respect for, reality. It is a (r)evolution which would like to design mechanisms for handling the demands set by reality.

This (r)evolution towards a respect for the two poles of reality is a purging process for the Afrikaner through which he will once again find his political balance in the truth.

3. The Structures and Growth Potential of Association-Politics

The first structure to be designed by Afrikaner politics in a new dispensation is the consociation between whites, Coloureds and Indians. Because they have no country of their own and because their numbers, culture, interests and aims are compatible and in balance with each other, political power-sharing is practicable in a unitary state.

Own say in this consociation is evinced in own local authorities for each group, an own House in Parliament where own affairs are managed, and own areas, amenities and institutions.

Joint say is evinced in common structures in metropolitan councils, regional councils, a common parliament, a mixed cabinet and total participation in decision-making, legislation and executive power.

This consociation is, in fact, a type of federation which has the growth potential to develop more closely into a complete unitary state with possible integration on all levels, as a matter of personal choice. The compromise of ethnic differences in politics may fall away in a further (r)evolution.

The second structure of compromise-politics is the instituting of separate states for the black nations, each in its own country. The structure is based on historical facts, on the development that has already taken place in which four independent states have come into being, and on the compromise that the nation-state remains the basis of South African politics.

In this structure self-determination for each black nation is entrenched and the domination of blacks among themselves, or of black over white, is structurally eliminated.

The growth potential of these separate states to develop into reasonably prosperous socio-political-economic units is present, provided that co-operative projects, co-operative areas and a network of economic interaction is maintained between these states and South Africa.

The (r)evolution to a common economy for the whole of South Africa has already been achieved.

These states can also expand into a federation of black states where the concept of a unitary state may again be considered. Many blacks themselves may be against the idea because of a fear of domination.

The third structure of compromise-politics is the creation of autonomous municipalities for blacks outside their national states, especially for those in the urban areas of South Africa. This group has acquired the name 'urban blacks' although the term is, strictly speaking, too narrow a conccpt.

Through the devolution of power, local and territorial government will become practically autonomous governing bodies, just like the provinces in a federation.

It is not entirely impossible that the black people within the Republic may well become part of a fourth chamber in a federal parliament, as the fourth leg of the white-Coloured-Indian parliament. However, the Afrikaner is not receptive to this (r)evolution and there are valid reasons for this: the numerical imbalance (the urban blacks are by far the majority group in the Republic); the opposition from within their own lands where such a differentiation between urban and rural people, as an ethnic division, is seen as both forced and absurd.

Expanding the compromise by (r)evolution to include urban blacks in a unitary state which would form a confederal or federal association with the existing black states is a possibility promoted by both black and white (among them Afrikaners). It must, however, be stressed yet again that the National Party Afrikaner fears the disappearance of his self-determination in such an extreme compromise – and the fear is not groundless.

The fourth structure – and the (r)evolution towards this structure is well on its way – is metropolitan or regional government in which the four ethnic groups share in various ways. The municipalities of all four groups have a voice in an umbrella service organisation which, according to acceptable formulas, managerial and financial policies, supplies infra-structural services to the municipalities.

Here the growth potential is de-politicised regional government in joint bodies for the four ethnic groups.

The fifth structure is confederation on a national level, with the following participants: the Republic as a unitary state between three ethnic groups, the black states, and the blacks in the Republic, who are present as an entity in the confederation. This confederation will also have to clinch compromise-politics in the sense that it is less than the classic federation, and more than the classic confederation.

The compromise on one hand is that the South African confederation will retain the characteristics of a confederation, such as the retention of the sovereignty of each participating state, the approval of joint decisions made by the parliaments of autonomous members before such decisions become legally valid, consensus as a principle for decision-making and many other typical confederal definitions.

On the other hand, the confederation must have a firmer form content than the classic confederation by, among other things, establishing a Confederal State Council with its own symbols, secretariat and institutions, a Confederal Leaders' Forum which will function like a cabinet in joint affairs, a Confederal Agenda which will establish joint affairs, subject to joint decision-making, in a Confederal Agreement, and a Confederal Financing Policy in which the economically weaker black partners of the confederation will get entrenchments for satisfactory aid for development.

Alongside these structures giving form and shape to compromise-politics the disappearance of legal discrimination is essential.

This means that the fundamental laws of the old apartheid dispensation will have to be repealed – that is an essential part of compromise-politics. The laws relating to race classification, group areas, separate amenities, mixed marriages and immorality are the most important.

However, merely repealing the laws cannot be part of the compromise. The compromise also demands that the rights of ethnic groups and group relationships must be entrenched. Therefore, a mutually satisfactory law will have to be negotiated which will give legal status to the white/black/brown and grey spheres.

The complete establishment of compromise-politics lies in the future but sufficient political energy is operating among Afrikaners to present this model as a solution to the dispensation of nations.

At this stage – at least for the eighties – it is the furthest that Afrikaners will allow their (r)evolution to develop.

This compromise-model, whatever weaknesses, intricacies and vagueness it may contain, does represent a significant (r)evolution of political policy among Afrikaners.

In the pessimism over the irreconcilabilities in South African politics there is the single hope that the (r)evolution of compromise-politics between the two basic political concepts (the unitary state and the nation-states) will be the choice of all the groups concerned. This compromise-politics has been accepted by a significant number of Afrikaners and their majority will continue to grow.

It has also been accepted by a great many Coloureds and Indians as a starting point.

The burning question remains whether the blacks will accept it. There are signs of both hope and despair.

---

[1] Arnheim, M T W. *South Africa After Vorster*. Cape Town: Howard Timmins, 1979.

3 The (R)evolution of Religious Attitudes

1. Church and Nation

The prominent place of the church among Afrikaners is not unusual; wherever Christianity has been established in the world ecclesiasticism has resulted.

Other phenomena of the Christian world are also evident among Afrikaners – fragmentation in the church, defection, and increasing secularisation.

Despite this the Afrikaans churches have an exceptional status in the Afrikaans community, and an involvement with Afrikaner politics.

This involvement has an historical basis. Traditionally the church leader was also the community leader. The church leader identified completely with the Afrikaner urge for freedom, the fight for recognition of the Afrikaans language, the economic plight which so often threatened the Afrikaners as a group and, with the rejection of the Afrikaner's political policy by the world and other ecclesiastical communities, the church leaders sided with the Afrikaner.

The church was in the forefront in presenting a justifiable outlook on life for the philosophy of apartheid.

There was a time (luckily past although there are still glimpses of it) when Bible texts were used in an attempt to substantiate apartheid. Various biblical injunctions in the Old Testament demanding apartheid between Israel and other heathen nations were applied to the political situation in South Africa. Subtly, the Afrikaner nation was identified with the Chosen People as the carrier of the Divine message, as opposed to the black nations with their animistic religions. A great deal of time, money and attention was given to missionary work to bring the gospel to blacks but black converts were not accepted into the mother church. A separate church was established for them and later this policy was applied to Coloureds as well.

However, separate churches were not established with wholly 'evil racist motives'. In missionary history throughout the world separate churches were created because of differences in language, culture, personal forms of religious expression and an own community experience.

A further rationale for separate churches was the opinion, held in Calvinist circles, that the church did not erase national ties. The church evinces and reveals itself in each nation without disputing that nation's existence. The ideal, it was argued, was for each nation to have its own church and that the churches of the nations would protect the unity of the church on higher levels than the congregational by ecumenical means, where there would be contact between the various 'nation churches' of the same faith.

There was no mixing on congregational level and the 'white church' was closed to black membership and attendance. The 'grounds' for this were the above argument of separate churches in each nation, the separate living areas and the differences in civilised standards. Another motive which plays a part – even if it is not easily admitted – is colour prejudice. This is evidenced by the fact that even today there are still heated discussions on the subject and incidents are still recorded where blacks are shown the door at white churches when they wish to attend services, special days of prayer and funerals. This rigid approach to the colour bar in the church undeniably reveals colour prejudice.

This attitude has slowly softened but the basic tenets of church apartheid are still adhered to by the Afrikaans churches.

The churches also provided a rationale for the political policy of separateness. The argument runs thus: the political policy in South Africa calls upon the biblical principles of the diversity of nations as a premise, and each nation is destined to maintain and evolve that which is his own.

Group rights, group freedom and group identity are justified, as long as you give unto others what you demand for yourself. The policy of separateness wants to achieve precisely that: it wants to protect all nations in South Africa against domination, suppression, exploitation and obliteration and wants to give them an opportunity to evolve.

The basic plan of the philosophy of apartheid is order, justice, freedom, self-expression and self-preservation. Therefore it is justified in the religious ethic. There are extensions of the policy, such as racism and discrimination, which must be combated, but the fact that it manifests itself in an imperfect reality does not make the roots of the policy bad.

The Afrikaans churches are consensus churches when it comes to the philosophy of separate development.

On the other hand, there are confrontation churches in South Africa which reject this policy as un-Christian. Among these churches there are many leaders of the so-called daughter churches – the black and brown churches of the Dutch Reformed (NGK) Church and other Afrikaans churches – as well as English-speaking churches.

The confrontation churches present this argument: the root of the separate development policy is wicked because it is built on factors like race discrimination, power politics and the structural violence of the system by which the majority is suppressed by the minority. It is rooted in a superior chauvinism and a capitalist financial power.

In this polarisation between churches over political policy many sharp accusations are constantly hurled back and forth.

Many Afrikaans Christians say that the black, brown and English-speaking churches are turning their prophetic calling into political agitation, their priestly calling into social gospel and their Divine calling into a political pressure group.

The confrontation churches claim that the Afrikaans churches are politicised, disobedient to Christ, unwilling to bow before Him.

2. Protest in the Church

Apart from individual voices, like those of Dr Beyers Naude and his Christian Institute, there was little protest in the seventies against the attitude of the church towards separateness. The protesters were regarded as heretics and in effect banned from the churches.

The first signs of protest from members of the NGK establishments came at the end of 1980 when eight well-known NG theologians published a testimony in *Die Kerkbode*, the official mouthpiece of the NGK.

There were attempts to drive them into all kinds of corners and to hang labels on them, but their standing was too high to thwart their influence.

The core of their testimony is that the calling of the church should be one of reconciliation in South Africa's tense racial situation and it should play a more active role as reconciliator. The church must show more compassion and indignation over the poverty, humiliation, powerlessness, exploitation and discrimination experienced by black and brown communities. The church must work against alienation within its family of churches and the various 'colour churches' – black, brown and white – which all profess the same creed, should experience and evince a greater unity. The church must draw the sword against the sin of racism. The church has a reformatory calling with regard to the political order and systems and must therefore be active in its prophetic calling to change the politics in South Africa to meet the demands of the Bible.

This testimony resulted in plain speaking. Scarcely a year later, in November 1981, the book *Stormkompas*, written by twenty-four theologians and members of the NGK, appeared. Their protest was more extensive and more critical than that of the eight theologians.

Unfortunately there are contributions in the book which attack the church more from a political viewpoint than a considered biblical testimony. It made a strong impact, however, and gave great impetus to the protest discussion in the Afrikaans churches.

In the book the authority of the Bible as the only guide

for the church is stressed. The existence of a church, it states, is not built on binding factors like blood, territory, language or status. Church unity is part of the fabric of the church and in South Africa's multi-national composition that unity must be apparent. For this reason it is argued that the brown, black and white churches of the NGK should become one church, with allowances being made for the existence of separate 'language congregations'. The present existence of separate NG churches for the various population groups is an artificial and ideological division of people. The white NGK has become a middle-class church, defending the status quo, that is the group interests of the Afrikaner. A strong plea is made for the involvement of the church in the restoring of human rights and the combating of social injustice among the coloured population groups.

The policy of separate development does not satisfy the evangelical demand of justice and the Christian dare not merely endorse the policy. The authors also sharply criticise the silence of the church in the face of the hurtful results of the Group Areas Act and the biblically-unsupported Mixed Marriages Act and some aspects of the Immorality Act.

One of the summarised premises in the book states: 'The NGK must prepare its members for the fact that the white man obviously cannot rule South Africa alone indefinitely'.[1]

This protest gained further momentum when an open letter from 123 office-bearers of the NGK was published in June 1981.

In this letter, too, the accent falls heavily on the unity of the church which is primary and normative and, while the authors acknowledge the diversity, they regard this as secondary. The authors state adamantly that the church may have no other criterion for its membership than the profession of faith in Christ. Therefore separate churches as church policy is condemned. A strong demand is made for the opening of the doors of the church to all.

The open letter criticises the political system and its laws as symbols of alienation. It pleads that all people who regard South Africa as their fatherland should be involved in the planning of a new dispensation.

These three documents of protest, which appeared from the bosom of the church in the space of two years, signed by leading personalities in the church, are an indication of the extent and intensity of the (r)evolution of religious attitudes among the Afrikaners. This (r)evolution is affecting the formerly unassailable bastion of apartheid – the church-sanctioned, religious-ethical bases of separate development.

Everything in South Africa is politicised. This movement of the church to biblically-founded thinking about politics cannot escape the tentacles of the political octopus. Especially after the coarse and one-sided generalisations contained in a biting attack made at the Ottawa Conference of the World Alliance of Reformed Churches led by a brown NG minister, dr Allan Boesak, politics became part and parcel of the church.

The motivation to have apartheid declared a heresy was clearly politically inspired. The General Synod of the NGK, which met directly after Ottawa at the end of 1982, was seen by many to be politically inspired as well. There are also political overtones in *Stormkompas* and the open letter which evoked political reactions, instead of fundamental ones.

The question is whether politics or pure biblical-ecclesiastical considerations will have the last word in the expanding protest in the church.

Those members of the Afrikaans churches who are already in the throes of the (r)evolution of political attitudes and policies will only be stimulated by the church protest, and the ecclesiastical protesters will be stimulated by political shifts and changes in attitude.

It can safely be forecast that the church protest will grow but also that polarisation in the church is inevitable.

All this forms an essential part of the Afrikaner (r)evolution which is striving towards a new dispensation which can be justified biblically. If the (r)evolution succeeds in legalising the new politics theologically, the spadework will have been done for the successful execution of the Afrikaner (r)evolution.

3. Perspective on the Church Debate

Unbelievable arrogance, Pharisaism and scandalous acts have been committed in the name of Christ – the history is there for all to read.

The church as evil is also a great truth; the existence of the church is part of imperfection. Murder and the bearing of false witness have taken place in the church, unholy revolutions initiated and justifiable revolutions suppressed. A measure of healthy scepticism is essential when one looks at the church and its pronouncements.

The fact that consensus churches and confrontation churches both call on the Bible to back their viewpoints increases this scepticism. The Bible is obviously not a political handbook with clearcut patterns for national policies.

The interpretation of the Bible must also be taken with a pinch of salt because the mood of the time, situation and accent also affect biblical interpretation.

It is a good starting point to say that all churches, and spokesmen for churches, in South Africa, by virtue of the general fact of evil, one-sidedness and an acceptance of different and differing realities, should not be too haughty in their belief that they know precisely what the Lord's will is for our political system.

Not that the church doesn't have the right, or the duty, to be politically involved. The Word which the church serves has authority on all levels and that is why the Word-church also has a say in all things, including politics.

There are criticisms, doubts and suspicions surrounding the viewpoints of the confrontation churches.

How do they arrive at the conclusion that a system of one man, one vote, in a unitary state, is God's commandment for South Africa?

How do they reconcile the fact that so many of the churches' spokesmen are filled with hate, negativism, despair and rancour?

The threat that they will, out of protest, incite people to break the laws of the land, is suspect, and the pleas for boycotts and the endorsement of violence is gravid with revolution.

A politicised theology is at work, operating from a specific political ideology against Afrikaner politics. It is an agitation which is loading the Christian truths and concepts with an explosive which is alien to the Bible.

There is also such a thing as theological arrogance, which puts forward as the supreme truth only those things which suit one.

There must, after all, be understanding for the Christian motivation of Afrikaners in affairs like national identity, group rights, own ethnic churches and the good fruits which the policy of separate development bore. This terrible reproach against the Afrikaner, which only serves to blind them, strengthens the suspicion that these are hostile African drums which are being beaten.

The voices of protest within the confrontation churches and also those within the Afrikaner churches occasionally irritate because the Lord, the Bible and all the pure words of eternity are reserved for the 'suffering black people of God'. The Afrikaner and his church are the 'dark sinners' who will be declared anathema, to be dismissed as lepers from the benign presence of God.

When the Bible rains judgement on the Pharisees, not only the Afrikaners get wet.

The consensus churches of the Afrikaner are not free from criticism.

Godless apartheid caricatures were created over the years, witness to a self-righteousness and dishonesty of a white theology which tried to bend the church to serve white interests.

Appalling racism is accepted in the churches.

There are many question marks hanging over the political involvement of these churches. Too often it seems like an afterthought, a glossing over, an avoidance of controversy, a ducking of choices, a fear of straight talking, a formal correctness and officialdom without a really incisive conviction about the necessity for renewed justice for South Africa.

The churches have become too much nation-church, ethnic-church, Afrikaner-church, for whom their own group prejudice has become their measuring stick.

Against this politicised background, which is present in the churches of both camps, scepticism is justified.
However, a meaningful change is taking place in the Afrikaner churches. A sensitivity to the demands for justice is developing which is a part of the Afrikaner (r)evolution of the eighties. It represents an awakening conscience and a protesting indignation about three specific issues.

– The unacceptability of racial separation in the churches of the Afrikaner, which protests the closed church door for black and brown Christians and members of the NGK at white services; which protests against the separation between mother church (white) and daughter churches (black and brown); which protests against the lack of unitary experience and the alienation from one another.
This (r)evolution does not want to do away with own language churches and group churches *per se*. It is a (r)evolution against their being enforced.
– There is protest against the political involvement of the church with the Afrikaner government which creates the impression that the Afrikaner church condones a political policy and refuses to adhere to the biblical injunctions in opposing certain apartheid laws which are unholy in all aspects.
– There is protest about the church's neglect of the calling to conciliate and to conciliate in such a way that the conciliation of races can be seen as a new move towards political and social justice. The church involves itself too little with the identification of the needs of black and brown people in a discriminatory society.
 The (r)evolution is based on the level of theological interpretations and an evaluation of the present policy of separate development, and the manner in which it was applied in the life of the church.

---

[1] Smith, N J (editor). *Stormkompas*. Cape Town: Tafelberg Publishers, 1981. Premise 38, p 140.

4 The (R)evolution and Afrikaner Organisations

1. Organisations, Academics, Businessmen, Radio and Television

Apart from politics and the church, Afrikaners are active over a wide spectrum in various institutions.

The most important of these are the Afrikaner-Broederbond and the Ruiterwag, education as represented in organised teachers' organisations, parents' associations and church organisations as well as schools and universities, organisations dealing with interests such as the Suid-Afrikaanse Akademie vir Wetenskap en Kuns, the Afrikaanse Handelsinstituut, the Federasie van Afrikaanse Kultuurverenigings and the Rapportryers.

Afrikaans authors, Afrikaans theatre and Afrikaans radio, television and press are important facets of Afrikaner self-projection and self-awareness.

These institutions, apart from the few rebels who knocked on the doors over the years, were and are the carriers of the established Afrikaner outlook on and attitudes to life. In the past these institutions were steeped in the ethos of isolation, the ethnic the overriding principle, with its ideology of apartheid and practices of separation, and the pivotally-contained energy which exclusively projected the Afrikaner nation as the core-nation.

Although the central motives of the Afrikaner (r)evolution are active here – after all, there are only about two million Afrikaners and the top leaders are, of necessity, members of all the sectors – there is, with the exception of businessmen, a great deal of opposition to the (r)evolution in these sectors.

Within the institutions a struggle for the soul of the Afrikaner is taking place. The result of the fermentation of the

verligte and verkrampte orientation is as yet undecided.
The church and education are strongly represented in organised culture and they are the chief advocates of the Afrikaner concepts of the fifties and sixties.

At universities various Afrikaner academics were, however, leaders of the reform with their contributions in discussion groups, publications, speeches and newspaper articles. They remain an important influence.

An estimated minus 40 per cent of university Afrikaners, both lecturers and students, are actively against the (r)evolution, while a plus 60 per cent have arrived at the (r)evolution or are on their way to it. Afrikaans students, as the leaders of the next generation, will build the bridge to the new era. Confronted with the realities of the year 2000, and conditioned by the changing attitudes which distinguish the present era, their choice will unavoidably round off the (r)evolution.

The academics' contribution is their provision of the scientific rationale for the necessity of change. Prominent economists deliver reasoned speeches on labour integration and interwoven economic activities against which a passion for economic and labour apartheid stands no chance. The renovated labour laws, based on the report of the academic Nic Wiehahn, are a concrete example. They brought a large section of the Afrikaner nation to an acceptance of the labour bargaining right of blacks in the trade union movement, the mixed factory floor, the setting aside of job reservation, the easing of influx control of blacks into industrial areas and parity in pay, rights and facilities.

The input from demographers pointed to population numbers, population shifts and the irreversible process of urbanisation. It was convincingly proven that socio-economic realities must have an influence on a changing political dispensation – a dispensation which can no longer accommodate many of the old apartheid slogans.

The political scientists stimulated many fruitful discussions about constitutional patterns, the unsuitability of the Westminster system for the composition of South Africa's population, the dangers of confrontation and isolation politics, and the options among which a choice had to be made with all due speed.

Over the past few years theologians, ethicists, historians, sociologists etcetera, have constantly been in the spotlight with perspectives and research results which, step by step, presented the Afrikaner with the challenge of the politics of reform.

The Afrikaner (r)evolution can be traced directly back to the popularisation and application of the findings of academics of high status. Apart from their contributions in the media and the generous space granted them, many of the academics are also sought after speakers in organisations like the Rapportryers.

In Afrikaner business circles political conservatism is definitely waning. The present generation of businessmen is at the forefront of reform. This is a significant fact in the light of the shift in professional status in the Afrikaner community. The businessman, and the professions, have replaced teachers and ministers of the church as 'prestigious people'. They have grown in status and authority to become important pacesetters.

Today one finds 'Afrikaner princes' – men with charisma, influence, success, authority and symbolic status – not in the circles of the conservative movement but at the forefront of the (r)evolution.

Radio and television have made an enormous contribution in establishing Afrikaner self-respect. The media is not a deliberate part of the (r)evolution. On the contrary, from time to time there has been serious criticism from the P W Botha government about the so-called 'half-hearted and over-cautious SABC' which does not actively support the reform movement. The criticism led to action when a senior civil servant was appointed as head of the SABC with the unstated intention that he should see to it that radio and television 'co-operated' in the battle to win the hearts and minds of the people for the new politics.

A great deal of the governmental pressure on the SABC has to do with the temptation faced by all governments to use the powerful electronics of television for the furtherance of their own policies, and efforts to exercise stricter control are rationalised with the argument that the SABC is an organisation controlled by law.

The deliberate and forced involvement of the SABC with the politics of the day, with the aim of either promoting or criticising political trends is counter-productive. That the SABC cannot ignore the (r)evolution, or the forces which are accomplishing it, is also true. Without losing its position of trust and objectivity, the SABC is compelled to mirror the great debate in South Africa and, in a manner that is informative, provides and influences perspective.

This (r)evolution-actuality must, of necessity, expand in the SABC programmes and it forecasts a further consolidation of the (r)evolution.

The contribution of the SABC has thus far been rooted in the expansion of the Afrikaner experience, of his language and his capabilities. Positive self-awareness is essential for a nation in transition and the SABC built up that self-awareness. There is a demonstrative nationalism, a propagandistic nationalism and a lump-in-the-throat nationalism. All three have a time and a place. The SABC should not allow itself to be seduced into presenting all three nationalisms as this would be counter-productive.

Instead N P van Wyk Louw should perhaps be used as a guide to the nationalism which must assist in making the (r)evolution a reality.

[While] nationalism does not exclude politics it also includes far more than politics. It is a heartfelt identification with everything that happens within a nation; a love for the things which make a nation more proud and more aware, which also makes it materially stronger; it is compassion for its suffering and a struggle against everything that makes it suffer; it is a bitter hatred for everything small in a nation and for everything which affects its pride and humiliates it. It is the determination to do whatever lies within one's power and without thought of gain, to enrich the spiritual possessions of a nation.[1]

59

Van Rensburg (*Swewende Ewewig*) finds the following accents in Van Wyk Louw's national feeling:

The national experience of belonging to a young, small, threatened nation.

Questioning nationalism as a kind of loving familial infighting.

The nationalism of compassion. 'One loves a nation not because it is wonderful and the best nation on earth; you love it because of its wretchedness.'[2]

The nationalism of humility which is modest, not ostentatious.

The nationalism of association with your country and its people.

The nationalism of existence-in-justice which creates a living space which is open and allows freedom to enjoy a fulfilled and unoppressed life. Being a nation is no sectarian affair.

Back to the SABC. If this nationalism of N P van Wyk Louw's can be transmitted by means of radio and television it will be a great contribution to the Afrikaner (r)evolution.

Afrikaners must develop insight into our smallness, our isolation and threatened state; into our wretchedness which evokes compassion and love for the needs of our time; old certainties must be questioned and new perspectives must be given for an existence-in-justice.

To sow and nurture this seed is the work of an expert. The propagandist must not be allowed to beat his drums or to open his box of his tricks on radio and television.

To accompany the (r)evolution demands a deep felt acquiescence.

2. *The Afrikaner-Broederbond (AB)*

Here the important question is: where does the AB stand in this (r)evolution? This organisation, with its 13 000 members, has great influence, especially in matters on philosophies of life.

The exposure during 1982 of this organisation through newspaper reports, whispering campaigns and church debates even made headlines overseas. It is interesting to note that important overseas visitors to South Africa are quick to ask questions about the role of the AB in the decision-making processes of the country's administration. The popular questions – and they hide an allegation – are the following:

* What influence and hold does the AB have on the Government, its political policy and political decisions?
* Is the AB a conservative and chauvinist power which promotes the Afrikaner cause at the expense of other nations? In other words is the AB a discriminatory factor?
* What hold does the AB have on the Afrikaans churches?
* Why a secret organisation?
* Does the AB manipulate all branches of South African society by planting its members in a network of influential posts and then putting pressure on them and controlling them from a central bureau of power?

The most comprehensive published documents on the AB are Ivor Wilkins' and Hans Strydom's *The Super-Afrikaners*[3] and A N Pelzer's *Die Afrikaner-Broederbond: Eerste 50 Jaar.*[4]

Both claim to be objective reports on the history, viewpoints and functions of the AB but there are justifiable reservations about both books. *The Super-Afrikaners* was written by two outspoken opponents of the AB, and their sources were intercepted and leaked documents of the organisation. They had to project a complete picture which was made up of bits and pieces and one cannot help suspecting, therefore, that the book is incomplete and prejudiced. It wants to be investigative journalism with all the accompanying sensationalism. Pelzer's book was written on the instruction of the AB. Distrust is perhaps understandable because it is possible that only selected and chosen material has been used. In any case, this book is primarily an historical review containing little of the present day activities of the AB.

The Super-Afrikaners starts with an introduction which immediately sets out to establish suspicion that the AB rules in all possible sectors. Prime ministers, the cabinets since the time of Dr Malan, executives in the civil service, the SABC, and in big institutions like Iscor, Sasol, Sanlam and the Afrikaans press, are all members of the AB. The rectors of virtually all Afrikaans, Coloured, Indian and black universities are also Broeders.

The inevitable conclusion is that the AB is the power behind every throne.

The history of the AB is discussed in broad outline and then attention is focused on specific standpoints of the AB. These standpoints are construed from excerpts from AB documents and quotes from public speeches of AB members. This is a very unreliable method; there is no investigation as to whether the viewpoints expressed by AB members, whether in or outside the AB, reflect the official policy of the AB or are merely personal points of view. Little attention is given to development or changes in attitudes.

The premise in these chapters dealing with AB standpoints is obvious.

It must be 'proven' that the AB sees the English-speakers in South Africa as enemies, that the AB attitude towards Coloureds is isolation from the whites, that the Verwoerdian concept of apartheid is still the leitmotiv of the AB, that the AB is a collaborator in restrictions and bannings and that 'the Broederbond remains an inherent, powerful and abiding presence within the soul of the Afrikaans Church'.[5]

They speak about 'oaths before each other and God'.[6]

The Broederbond 'developed an obsession with Afrikanerdom, that it must be protected, promoted and that it must rule'.[7]

'Nationalist politicians are fond of repeating, correctly, from public platforms that South Africa is a plural society, a society of various cultures and races. They earnestly tell their public audiences, correctly, that any solution to South Africa's complex problems must take account of this political reality. Yet how much confidence can one place in the sincerity of their proclaimed desire to find an equitable accommodation for all the elements of the population, when one knows that they are secretly pledged to serve the exclusive interests of Afrikanerdom? How much faith can there be in their public utterances of conciliation, when one knows, or suspects, that in secret conclave the real commitment remains Afrikaner domination? It seems inevitable that while the Broederbond lurks beneath the political surface in South Africa, any moves towards dialogue will be fraught with suspicion and mistrust.'[8]

'When the Afrikaans Church pronounces on matters of national importance, it is influenced by the Broederbond, to which most of its members belong.'[9]

A N Pelzer's book contains a great deal of historical data with the accent on the fact that a development in thinking is taking place within the AB.

He quotes the following investigations which were undertaken to evaluate the AB: the commission for Actuality Problems of the Council of Churches; the Jan Oelofse investigation for the Hervormde Kerk; a commission of the Gereformeerde Kerk; the investigation of Judge D H Botha, commissioned by Dr Verwoerd.

He points out that the investigators were not members of the AB, that they acted according to accepted investigative norms and that their findings were all positive.

In his discussion of the activities of the AB he mentions the fact – and he gives documentary proof – that the AB, as guardian of the Afrikaner's culture, emphasised the necessity of close co-operation between Afrikaners and English-speakers, especially after the Republic was established, and that the attitude to non-whites was put in a positive light while Afrikaners were warned to abandon their prejudices in favour of a realistic attitude of co-operation.

He also outlines in detail the AB's contribution to Afrikaner achievement economically, politically and socially.

Many of the questions formulated at the beginning of this article are answered by Pelzer from an historical perspective.

The AB must be sunk without trace if it is true that it is a pressure clique, intriguing in secret; if its aim is the creation of jobs for pals; if it wants to play Superdad, manipulating people, institutions, churches, campuses, governments, in fact everything under the sun; if it is a sanhedrin of conceited Afrikaners who declare general anathema if the road it has prescribed is not followed; if it is a sick, ritualistic group which, by all kinds of ceremonies, inflates its members to breathless pomposity ...

If all this were true, the AB would have no right to exist. It would be an offence and wholly unacceptable were 13 000 men secretly to govern the country. It would be completely opposed to the principles of democracy. It is dangerous and borders on the possibility of corruption.

The basic question is, is it true?

I have enough grounds to maintain quite the opposite and submit the following arguments:

The Afrikaner's outlook on life and the world puts a high premium on sovereignty and freedom of the individual and of institutions. Such a super-organisation, serving as an umbrella over other independent institutions, is wholly alien to the philosophy of the Afrikaner. Nor will the character of the Afrikaner permit it. He is geared to being his own master. It is absurd to claim that the moderator of the NGK, a prime minister or members of the cabinet, a newspaper head, a businessman, a rector, a headmaster, you name it, would allow himself to be prescribed to, manipulated or called to account by a small group of men at the head of the AB. And to claim that the AB would poke its nose into or demand a say in decision-making in other agendas or instances is equally absurd.

I would like to make the point that, both in theory and in practice, a strong sense of territorial frontiers is active in the AB, in that it respects the independent functioning of other institutions. There is also a strong sense of freedom which operates from the viewpoint that its members must act according to their instincts, their consciences and their responsibility in various arenas. It is nonsense to allege that censorship of thought is applied or that there is constant interrogating of members.

The AB accepts heterogeneity of viewpoint as part of its composition, as long as its members demonstrate and respect their integrity as Afrikaners.

The influence of the AB does not lie in its interference and proscription but rather in its shaping and honing of the attitudes of its members. The AB is a think-tank where people can combine their talents to evaluate the issues of the day. It is a philosophy-debate, a facts-debate, a research-debate and all the findings are disseminated and discussed among members. With the combined results of the think-tank, meetings are arranged and influence is applied to authorities and powers within the community.

Is such a think-tank and its resultant influencing activity wrong?

I would say no. It is the right of any group – and many make use of this right – to debate issues and to submit their findings where they are applicable.

If the results of your debate are representative of an influential group, you will obviously achieve bargaining power. Businessmen, the professions, interest groups and others daily achieve consensus among their members and put their findings before decision-makers. The Afrikaner, as an identifiable group, surely has the same right, and the better his bargaining power, the better he functions – that is a generally valid democratic reality. Such think-tanks cannot be resented because they think in an organised fashion; they must be measured by the content of their thoughts.

It is important to establish the thought content of the AB because that content will indicate whether the (r)evolution of Afrikaner thought is also taking place in that prestige organisation.

What is being thought has a certain time limit. I will grant that the AB, within a framework of time, was and is a child of its time. Circulars, speeches and policy statements from the year dot can be dug up which will reflect the sentiments and actualities of that era.

The test is whether the AB has a breadth of vision concerning the problems which we are experiencing in the present era.

There is a positive reply to this question.

* As far as colour policy is concerned, the view is that discrimination is unacceptable, that the association of nations in an equal consociation is essential, that joint

responsibility in decision-making on communal affairs is the key to a future dispensation, that it may never occur at the expense of authority over own affairs, that confederation is a usable starting-point for the accommodation of black joint responsibility in South Africa and that on all levels separateness and communality will ensure the future of South Africa.
* The great democratic principles of political rights, justice and freedom for all are the starting-point of the AB. The focus on Afrikaner affairs is in no way an exclusive and sectarian attitude of the AB. Other national groups are not deprived of their own interests in favour of the Afrikaner. On the contrary, the AB acknowledges the interdependence of our different national groups and that domination of one over the other should be rejected. Rather we should make common cause of development on various levels without threatening one another's identity and freedom.

The author finds no evidence for the distorted and sinister picture painted of the AB.

There is no evidence for the suspicion that the AB employs undemocratic principles in the exercise of its self-imposed aims.

There is no evidence for the suspicion that the AB exercises power over its members in important positions, making them dance to its tune in political and other spheres. Experience has proven the exact opposite. I find no evidence to prove the allegation that the AB is archaic in its attitudes to current affairs in South Africa. On the contrary, the AB is occupied with a highly modern agenda.

There is no evidence for the fears that the AB is racist and chauvinist. Although the Afrikaner nation is its defined area of operation, its involvement is with the complexities of South Africa and its basic concept is that agreement in justice, involving all nations, offers the only honourable solutions. Critical questions are self-evident.

Certainly the AB could review unnecessary secrecy because it gives unnecessary offence. Without becoming wholly public, it can find a balance between openness and confidentiality.

The AB must constantly guard against its members becoming involved on the local level in local in-fighting, pettiness, authoritarianism and manipulatory practices. This remains an ever-present possibility and the AB leadership should be mindful of it.

The AB must work against all signs of empire-building and must strongly emphasize the freedom and competence of each independent individual and institution. Although it is the declared point of departure the idea of sovereignty in own affairs must rise like yeast through the organisation.

This applies to the church, politics, education and all other structures in the community.

As the internal influence of the Afrikaner corps, the AB must always be able to pass the test that it uses its influence in a realistic, modern, mature and balanced manner according to the demands of the time. When necessary, it must publicly declare this.

If the AB takes care to be a renovative energy for a small nation with enormous responsibilities, it can play a creative role for the whole of South Africa.

If the (r)evolution can break through Afrikaner attitudes, make its way into the political policies of the Afrikaner and into church debates, it will inevitably also affect Afrikaner organisations.

---

[1] Van Wyk Louw, N P. *Berigte te Velde*. Cape Town: Tafelberg Publishers, 1971, p 64.
[2] Van Rensburg, F I J. 'Liberale Nasionalisme'. In *Swewende Ewewig*. Cape Town: Tafelberg Publishers, 1975, pp 22–3.
[3] Wilkins I and Strydom, H. *The Super-Afrikaners: Inside the Afrikaner-Broederbond*. Johannesburg: Jonathan Ball Publishers, 1978.
[4] Pelzer, A N. *Die Afrikaner-Broederbond: Eerste 50 Jaar*. Cape Town. Tafelberg Publishers, 1979.
[5] Wilkins, I and Strydom, H. *Op cit*, p 24.
[6] *Ibid*, p 443.
[7] *Ibid*, p 446.
[8] *Ibid*, p 447.
[9] *Ibid*, p 448.

5 The (R)evolution and the Afrikaans Press[1]

1. Newspapers Influence Public Opinion

It is an old debate – do newspapers have any real influence on public opinion and public life?

There are two points of view: newspapers determine and manipulate the attitudes of their readers and can even radically change their attitudes. The second viewpoint holds that newspapers can, at most, only reinforce or weaken existing attitudes by reflecting them.

Research into these two points of view has been done sporadically. The results proving that newspapers possess few powers of persuasion have been divergent. The problem, however, lies in the fact that most of the research has been done overseas, with special reference to the influence of newspapers on election results.

I think it is true that newspapers strongly influence public opinion. There is interaction between newspapers and public opinion on two levels. Public opinion has an effect on newspapers and newspapers have an effect on public opinon. In the first place newspapers give expression to the desires and expectations of the public. Newspapermen often use the expression 'tell the readers what they want to know'. To a large extent public preferences, dislikes, tastes and demands determine the supply.

Newspapers, however, also affect public opinion.

Public opinion reflects a combination of viewpoints on questions of general interest and its influence on those in a decision-making position.

Involved processes are at work in these spheres of influence and influence is not always measurable.

However, it remains a safe assumption, backed by

experience, that newspapers as shapers of public opinion definitely influence the political situations in a country. Watergate in the United States and Muldergate in the Republic are perfect examples.

The influence of newspapers is narrowly bound up with the stature of their editors and columnists. In a democracy the crusading newspaper is acknowledged as an essential cog in the machine of the system, as a competent partner in the political debate, as an authoritative evaluator of policies, arguments and trends. Carlyle's words are still valid: 'There are Three Estates in Parliament; but in the Reporter's Gallery yonder, there sat a fourth estate ...'

All true newspapers (as opposed to smaller publications which are neutral and primarily serve as advertising media) are crusading newspapers which advocate definite points of view on current affairs. The readers of a commentary, especially political commentary, are estimated at about ten per cent of readers, but they are usually intensely involved in the subject under discussion. That is why newspaper commentary plays a dynamic role in the strengthening and creation of attitudes held by the moulders of public opinion. The newspaper acts as leader of the discussion. The message of political leaders is transmitted to the nation. The questions, fears, resistances and expectations of the nation are communicated to the leaders. The discussions within the public body on matters of mutual concern, with all the different emphases, are given a voice in the newspaper. There is an on-going dialogue with the opponents of the newspaper's political policy.

In this role as leader of the discussion, the newspaper is a critic of the way policy is formulated and of its execution. It is an interpreter of undercurrents in political policy, a pioneer seeking new policy developments and a reinforcer of those political attitudes with which its readers agree.

The newspaper reading public is continually exposed to the newspaper angle on the news of the day. Its information is the only source (apart from radio and television) on which the reader can draw. Inevitably the newspaper shapes the reader's knowledge of the news.

Newspapers are the carriers of current practices on various levels – relaxation, fashion, housing etc. The newspaper attracts interest in, gives attention to and encourages awareness of certain practices. This also applies to politics. If the 'in thing' is a resistance to petty apartheid, the newspapers condition their readers by means of psychological effects of repetition.

Newspapers are the creators of climate, doing pioneering work by stimulating conscious or sub-conscious processes in the shaping of public opinion.

Through publicity, newspapers give status to certain issues, people, organisations or viewpoints, or the very opposite. The acceptance of an issue or a person is either promoted or criticised.

Although the credibility of the press condemns propaganda as a newspaper technique, newspapers, consciously or subconsciously, do campaign on certain issues, whether it be by deliberate repetition and prominence or by the projection of certain pet ideas of an editor or journalist.

The Afrikaans newspapers – as well as the English-speaking ones – have made a very definite contribution to the Afrikaner (r)evolution. They were part of the process.

2. *The Press and Change*

It is an open question whether the English press is basically motivated to bring about evolutionary political change in South Africa.

As an outspoken opposition press, they reject the political system of the Afrikaans community and therefore their argument is generally a plea for the rejection of the system, for a radical new political philosophy, instead of for a reformation of the existing system.

Where they do show any sympathy for reform initiatives, it is generally qualified as acceptable only because they are a step in the right direction. This change of direction is towards a system of universal vote in a unitary state according to the classic federation model.

It is doubtful whether the PFP-supported press has made any progress worth mentioning in selling their philosophy to their readers, because election results prove the contrary. In fact, reader resistance is clearly shown in the progress made among English-speakers by a politically conservative newspaper like *The Citizen*.

The negative role in which reform initiatives are denigrated and opposition mustered against them has already been referred to. It is more than a suspicion that this attitude has greatly contributed to the resistance to reform, especially among black and brown people.

The paradox, however, lies in the fact that the English-speaking press – in opposition – have made singular contributions to political change in South Africa.

When the Afrikaans newspapers during the early sixties, and earlier, were conspicuously devoted to sectional Afrikaner interests, Afrikaner politics and National Party policy, the English-speaking press propagated the existence of a total South African society.

The living conditions, problems, aspirations and frustrations of the black and brown communities were ceaselessly spotlighted. South Africa was kept fully informed that these communities were a political factor which had to be accommodated. By communicating the demands of black and brown and representing their interests, the English-speaking press sensitised South Africa to the necessity for change.

By throwing the spotlight on black poverty, inadequate housing, gross discriminatory laws and practices, the rise of black nationalism and increasing polarisation, they prepared the way for the politics of change which has as its object a racial dispensation which must also be acceptable to black and brown.

By communicating black opinion, they made South Africa aware of the actual voice of opposition in our politics.

By accenting the economic unacceptability of certain facets of the policy of separate development, they furthered the broadening of the policy which definitely initiated change, for example with regard to the decentralisation policy, influx control and the sharing of amenities.

The traditions of the West – democracy, the Rule of Law, the freedom of the press etc – were chosen as aggressive themes by the English-speaking press against narrowing influences, and as a result the public and its leaders were confronted with the political philosophy of freedom and justice, which in turn created a climate for resistance against closed systems.

The contribution of these newspapers in jolting their Afrikaans colleagues into an awareness of the need to place journalistic freedom above slavish submissiveness must not be underestimated. Their example did, after all, in the background, affect the emancipation of the Afrikaans newspaper.

Although the English-speaking press has little or no influence on Government decision-making, they are, as effective opposition, instruments for change because they outline the other side of the coin so clearly.

As to the Afrikaans press ...

Owing to the history of their origin, but also out of free choice, all the Afrikaans national newspapers allied themselves with the framework of National Party policy.

The process of emancipation from any form of National Party domination or voice in editorial policy has come a long way. The Afrikaans newspapers have been able to save their credibility and freedom in their independent political journalism without damaging their ties with Afrikaans political philosphy.

The political success story of the Afrikaans newspapers lies in the fact that in the Vorster era, against great opposition from the government and their own people, they initiated, supported and extended verligte trends. During the period 1972–1978 the Afrikaans press had to carry a heavy load by persevering with motivations for reform and change which went against the grain of many in the National Party.

The points that were strongly accented at that time were:

* The necessity of consultation with non-whites, as opposed to paternalism.

* That co-existence was a new concept in our common destiny as nations and that communality had to conquer compartmental thinking in new structures, a joint say in

politics and the sharing of amenities. The accent was placed on association politics and 'petty apartheid' was fought tooth and nail.

* The plea for a new constitutional dispensation with equal emphasis on a say in own affairs and joint affairs was constantly stressed and consolidated in the confederation concept and the federation concept for whites, Coloureds and Indians.

* The acceptance of the urban blacks as permanent and acceptance of the need for their own say over own affairs, plus the necessity of higher political structures for them. Referring them to the homelands as their political homes was simply not adequate.

* Moving away from discrimination and the revision of discriminatory laws, eliminating job reservation, equal labour bargaining power for non-whites and reform in black and brown education were prominent themes.

* The so-called normalisation of sport by the elimination of many of the barriers.

* The dangers of international isolation and the necessity of being of service to Africa.

Naturally no newspaper can formulate a policy but as a critic, a motivator and an interpreter it can create a climate for reform. Already during the tenure of John Vorster the Afrikaans press bore witness to a move towards a verligte political policy but it is P W Botha who symbolises the harvest for the Afrikaans press.

Flowing from the points mentioned above, the role of the Afrikaans press in the purging process within the National Party had a direct influence on change.

The first breakaway – that of Dr Albert Hertzog in 1969 – was strongly aided by the fearless journalism of the former Sunday newspaper *Die Beeld*. *Die Burger* and *Die Transvaler*, to a lesser degree, joined in. Afrikaans newspapers also helped prepare the way for the next split – that of Dr Andries Treurnicht in 1982 – by sharp criticism of rightwing efforts to frustrate the reformist politics and to hijack the National Party.

The political direction of the present administration undoubtedly has the general support of the prominent Afrikaans newspapers. The Prime Minister is seen as a positive reformer who is able to give strong impetus to the new dispensation. Not that the Afrikaans newspapers are uncritical. Virtually each week there are critical comments about certain affairs of state and a tendency to warn the Government not to hesitate while peering over its right shoulder.

However, Afrikaans newspapers oppose the course of the politics of total integration. The concept of separate development as a leitmotiv for our politics remains the prominent policy of the Afrikaans press. This is evident in the heavy emphasis on self-determination, an own living area for each group, and separate education.

The manner in which the Afrikaans press supports the reform politics at the moment is especially clear in its support for the idea of joining white, Coloured and Indian together in one state, with a mixed government built on separate local management committees. This is also made clear in the way in which it urges the implementation of the De Lange and the Rieckert reports, its concern about an agreement with the black nations and its advocacy of close confederal structures which will also give representation to urban blacks as a leg of the confederation, and its protest against any manifestation of colour discrimination.

The contribution of the Afrikaans newspapers to the furtherance of the Afrikaner (r)evolution is apparent on three levels.

The first is its straightforward, factual reporting on our political situation. In interviews, commentaries and news presentation it is evident that there is strong emphasis on the realities of numbers, economic demands and international involvement. By presenting the information prominently and continuously, these newspapers are making the Afrikaner ripe for responsible choices which are problem solving as opposed to ideologically directed.

Second is its almost intolerant handling of verkrampte approaches. The Afrikaans press succeeds in projecting verligtheid as the image of the responsible Afrikaner and verkrampheid as something deviant, dubious and disloyal to self. Verligtheid has acquired a decency, a prestige and a credibility, especially through the Afrikaans press.

This is a major contribution to a reformation momentum. In this respect there is the danger that this intolerance towards verkrampheid may lead to arrogance on the side of the Afrikaans newspapers, which in turn may be counter-productive to reformation. That is why the patient, sympathetic and reasoned argument, as a newspaper style, is preferable for Afrikaners who still hesitate to walk the reformation road. If the Afrikaner newspapers shout at those people who balk, the reaction will be certain. The Afrikaner is someone who must be won over step by step; there is no point in driving him with a whip.

In the third place the Afrikaans newspapers further the Afrikaner (r)evolution by focusing on Afrikaner institutions. The debate around the church, education, universities and their academics, the Broederbond and other organisations gets a great deal of prominence in these newspapers. Reformist ideas occupy many columns.

The question is whether the Afrikaans press is positively received by its public.

The answer is both yes and no. The yes is based on the fact that the credibility of Afrikaans newspapers is not disputed by many of its readers. They accept the bona fides of their newspaper as advocate for the Afrikaner cause, as spokesman for a dispensation of nations, and as watchdog of Afrikaner self-determination on all levels. They know their newspaper is no toothless lion, that it will snarl at the Government when necessary.

There is, however, a percentage of readers – and it may well be a significant percentage – which has a kind of hate relationship with Afrikaans newspapers. In the main they are Afrikaners with interests in and sympathy for the Conservative Party and the Herstigte Nasionale Party. They still read the Afrikaans newspapers because they have no real newspaper of their own and that is why they draw swords daily with the 'liberal Afrikaans press'. However, there are also National Party supporters who have reservations about the Afrikaans newspapers because they are 'not conservative enough'.

This tense relationship is not unusual and if the newspapers handle it correctly, they could increase their influence on those who are dissatisfied. The correct approach would be for newspapers to persist in the fearless promotion of new political attitudes.

The neo-colonialist approach of guardianship for which payment is the gratitude of non-whites must be argued against. Colour prejudice, colour isolation, colour entrenchment by law and colour anxiety, betraying a lack of belief in settlement, must be fought tooth and nail by the Afrikaans newspapers.

Change must be reflected in the columns as a positive fact, not merely as a strategy for survival.

The central theme of political journalism should be the absolute necessity of reaching a settlement for all nations in South Africa, and that this is only possible if a say over own affairs and a joint say over communal affairs for all of the people in South Africa is laid down in tight new structures.

It is doubtful whether a comprehensive, fully-fledged newspaper will be launched from the Treurnicht/Marais camp. It is too expensive and too risky an investment. Without the financial and other support from the extensive interests of press companies like Perskor and Naspers, such a newspaper would hardly be viable. These groups will remain embedded like flies in amber in political propagandist pamphlets like *Die Afrikaner* and *Die Patriot* unless they infiltrate and try to hijack an existing newspaper. Attempts in this direction are probably part of their strategy and there is no doubt that they will continue to manipulate and to be on the look-out for the opportunity to effect such a hijacking. Pressure groups do exist which try to inhibit existing newspapers in the hope of a takeover.

On the other hand, Afrikaans newspapers must be sensitive to the fact that they must serve the whole Afrikaans community and that they also have non-National Party Afrikaners as readers. This means that without diluting their political viewpoints they must avoid the deliberate humiliation of Afrikaners with opposing attitudes. The Afrikaans newspapers must also respect and promote the cultural ties and experience of all Afrikaners.

The reformist movement in politics cannot, however, lean too heavily on Afrikaans newspapers because Afrikaners are fairly indifferent newspaper readers. A great many Afrikaans families do not take in the message of Afrikaans newspapers simply because they either don't read them or only do so superficially. In any case, upper middle class Afrikaners, the backbone of the political reformist initiative, do receive the political message of Afrikaans newspapers.

The dilemma of the English-speaking newspapers is that while their pleas for radical change are alienating their white readers a more moderate approach would alienate their growing number of black readers. This ambivalence into which they have been led is affecting their credibility. The only solution would be to streamline newspapers until they have a clear-cut reading public.

In conclusion:

* Afrikaans newspapers played a key role, which they must maintain, in leading and accompanying the Afrikaner through the transitional phase to a new political dispensation. Their role is and will continue to be to confront the readers with the unavoidable facts of the South African reality and to point out that the only option for peace, prosperity and order is that of nation-association.
* However, the Afrikaans newspapers will only retain their influence as agents for change if they can project themselves as credible, rooted in the Afrikaans community, and serving the cause of the Afrikaner's right to self-determination. In all the outward thinking and movement which Afrikaans newspapers stimulate, they must remain pivotally-seeking if they want to serve the reformist politics.
* English-speaking newspapers will serve the cause of change if they abandon radicalism and negativism and accept the compromise, the compromise which says that

South Africa's new dispensation cannot be a unitary state but an association in which own say and joint say are entrenched by giving stature, in equal measure, to separateness and communality.

---

[1] This chapter has been taken largely from an RGN initiated publication entitled *Change in South Africa* and published by Butterworths in 1983, which contains an article by the author: 'The Press and Political Change in South Africa'.

Postscript

The Afrikaner (r)evolution ...
Is it wishful thinking, an overstrained expectation or a kind of supplication? Is it a reality which can be measured and tested? Is it an observation coloured by the lenses and filters of the author?

This book is probably a mixture of all three possibilities.

However, the forces are on the move.

Afrikaners are in transit to a new identity.

Isolation is being breached, there is a move away from racism, ethnicity as a divisive factor is being defused and an identification with co-existence is gaining momentum.

The shift in thinking exclusively of the Afrikaner to the realisation that he cannot go it alone is a meaningful movement to the centrifugal energy of a community of interests, cohesiveness and collectivity.

The relativisation of political options and the erosion of the original apartheid ideology among Afrikaners have paved the way for compromise politics, away from division as leitmotiv to a balanced formula of own say and joint say for all the peoples of South Africa on various terrains and government levels.

The process of dismantling the fundamental laws of the old apartheid dispensation is at work.

Within the Afrikaans churches the opposition to the (r)evolution is particularly strong but there are ample indications of a widening circle of protest against the white church door being closed to black and brown, against the alienation caused by colour within the family of the church, against the uninvolvement with political and social injustice and the theological condoning of the policy of apartheid.

The leaders of the Afrikaner nation in Afrikaans organisations are all beginning to agree that the central motives of the (r)evolution discussed in this book must be carried out.

A nation in the midst of such fluidity, and encouraged by its political leaders to make a breakthrough, can never be the same again.

This does not mean that on the road of choices, conflict among Afrikaners will not grow. The Afrikaner nation is doing a balancing act, leaving his old world of traditional political concepts and entering a new world, a world which is also dangerous. The excitement of the new world, however, is that it will open doors to something which historians will later describe as one of the wonders of the twentieth century.

This wonder will be the accommodation of races and nations in South Africa. The Afrikaner's balancing act is threatened by many forces aiming at his downfall.

The equilibrium can be disturbed if the pace is too slow – evolution on its own is too long a road and has lost its credibility. Immobility on this new road, either forced by or shocked into the total rejection of the Afrikaners' new initiatives by black and brown, may cause an explosive devolution process – and if the Afrikaner retreats, he will fall by the wayside and his downfall will not even be heroic.

To walk the (r)evolution road – and there is still a long way to go – is dangerous for the Afrikaner but it will have to be a calculated risk.

Only this Afrikaner (r)evolution can halt the rising black (r)evolution.

The adjustment to the (r)evolutionary course will demand that a great deal be relinquished.

This book underlines the hopes and the expectations, as well as the belief, that Afrikaners are tough survivors with a surprising ability, as shown in their history, to grow into a situation. They possess the clarity and levelheadedness to realise when they have arrived at a dead end, to persevere once a course has been chosen, and the capacity to follow as a group, if their leaders on all levels do not hesitate in the front ranks to pave the way to a future.

Their leaders are already part of the (r)evolution process

– leaders in politics, culture, the business sector, the professions and in the academic world. The Afrikaans press, radio and television are indivisibly committed to the breakthrough. And the youth, as the determining generation before the turn of the century, are motivated to solve South Africa's problems.

There is significant opposition to the (r)evolution among Afrikaners but the inevitable realities which are developing will be such a drawing power for the (r)evolution that the opposition will fade to a regional phenomenon which, seen in the context of the whole country, will represent at most one third of Afrikaners.

The non-Afrikaans white citizens have, by a convincing majority, opted for the (r)evolution, even if there are different accents. There are indications, however, that the new political model of the Afrikaner will gain acceptance by a large group.

Brown and black have definitely not come out against the Afrikaner (r)evolution, although a meaningful percentage are already radicalised and hope for a black revolution. The more the (r)evolution gets into its stride and delivers concrete results, however, the greater the drawing power will be among moderates in the coloured groups. And the moderates still have the leadership and the power bases to make choices. There is a willingness to compromise, and negotiations still bear good fruit. They will not buy hollow promises however. The Afrikaner (r)evolution will only gain enough support for co-operation if joint say is extended considerably beyond the classic confederation model.

Hope, expectation and confidence.

The following decade will be a breathholding time in which the contents of this book will either be confirmed or refuted.

Thereafter historians will sit in judgement on the wisdom or the stupidity of the Afrikaner nation.